DATE DUE

Demco, Inc. 38-293

At Issue

Should Cameras Be Allowed in Courtrooms?

Other Books in the At Issue Series:

At Issue

Should Cameras Be Allowed in Courtrooms?

Amanda Hiber, Book Editor

GREENHAVEN PRESS
A part of Gale, Cengage Learning

GALE
CENGAGE Learning·

Detroit • New York • San Francisco • New Haven, Conn • Waterville, Maine • London

7|08   # 193176989

GALE
CENGAGE Learning™

Christine Nasso, *Publisher*
Elizabeth Des Chenes, *Managing Editor*

© 2008 Greenhaven Press, a part of Gale, Cengage Learning.

Gale and Greenhaven Press are registered trademarks used herein under license.

For more information, contact:
Greenhaven Press
27500 Drake Rd.
Farmington Hills, MI 48331-3535
Or you can visit our Internet site at gale.cengage.com

For product information and technology assistance, contact us at

Gale Customer Support, 1-800-877-4253
For permission to use material from this text or product, submit all requests online at www.cengage.com/permissions

Further permissions questions can be emailed to permissionrequest@cengage.com

Articles in Greenhaven Press anthologies are often edited for length to meet page requirements. In addition, original titles of these works are changed to clearly present the main thesis and to explicitly indicate the author's opinion. Every effort is made to ensure that Greenhaven Press accurately reflects the original intent of the authors. Every effort has been made to trace the owners of copyrighted material.

Cover photograph reproduced by permission of Images.com/Corbis.

LIBRARY OF CONGRESS CATALOGING-IN-PUBLICATION DATA

Should cameras be allowed in courtrooms? / Amanda Hiber, book editor.
    p. cm. -- (At issue)
  Includes bibliographical references and index.
  ISBN-13: 978-0-7377-3928-2 (hardcover)
  ISBN-13: 978-0-7377-3929-9 (pbk.)
  1. Television broadcasting of court proceedings--United States. 2. Television broadcasting of news--Law and legislation--United States. I. Hiber, Amanda.
  KF8726.H53 2008
  347.73'12--dc22
                                     2008008895

Printed in the United States of America
1 2 3 4 5 6 7 12 11 10 09 08

Contents

Introduction

The debate over allowing cameras into America's courtrooms is hardly new. Most analysts trace the argument's origins to the 1965 Supreme Court case of *Billie Sol Estes v. Texas*. As journalist Al Tompkins writes, "Journalists and photographers covering that trial acted so outrageously that the Supreme Court slammed the door on cameras in the courts." It was not until 1981—"when cameras got quieter and needed no extra lights," Tompkins says—that the Supreme Court reconsidered its earlier decision and ruled that cameras in courtrooms were not inherently unconstitutional. As a result of this ruling, many states dropped their bans on cameras and other electronic media in courtrooms.

Court TV's debut in 1991 launched the age of the celebrity trial, according to many cultural observers. O.J. Simpson's infamous murder trial, in which the former football star was accused of killing his ex-wife and her friend, was televised from start to finish in 1995, and the public was a willing audience. As journalist Dahlia Lithwick reports, "An astonishing 91 percent of the television viewing audience watched the verdict." While the televised trial may have been a boon for ratings, many thought it trivialized the judicial process. Judge Lance Ito, who presided over the case, was criticized by many as surrendering control of his courtroom to the media. As a result, say numerous observers, restrictions on media access to courtrooms grew, particularly in high-profile cases. Writer Bob Egelko notes that since the Simpson trial "judges frequently have allowed TV at pretrial hearings, and sometimes for part of a trial, but never at one of the big, celebrity, tabloid-and-paparazzi cases—no Scott Peterson [convicted of killing his pregnant wife and unborn son], no Michael Jackson [entertainer acquitted of child molestation charges], no Robert Blake [actor acquitted of killing his wife]."

But in recent years, "the O.J. effect," as *Newsday* writer Tina Susman has deemed it, may have begun to wear off. In 2000, the Supreme Court allowed audio recordings of oral arguments in *Bush v. Gore* to be broadcast the same day. The high court has swiftly released tapes of other high-profile cases as well. There is even a growing movement to televise the Supreme Court itself, headed at the legislative level by Senators Arlen Specter (R-PA) and Chuck Grassley (R-IA), whose Sunshine in the Courtroom Act would require the televising of Supreme Court proceedings except in cases where violations of due process are foreseen.

The push to allow greater media access to courtrooms is seen by many as part of a larger cultural shift toward more media—and thus, more public—access to all aspects of American life. Alongside the Simpson trial, the 1990s saw the birth of the TV reality show, with MTV's *The Real World*, and the so-called trash talk shows, like *The Jerry Springer Show* and *The Maury Povich Show*. Tell-all memoirs like Kathryn Harrison's *The Kiss* and Mary Karr's *The Liar's Club* were best sellers, and the Weblog, or "blog," was born. To many cultural critics, the sum of these trends indicated a symbiotic growth of exhibitionism and voyeurism within American popular culture.

If this increasingly "confessional culture," as journalist Cristian Lupsa labels it, emerged in the 1990s, it had thoroughly infiltrated mainstream culture by 2000 and beyond. While *The Real World* maintained a cult following beginning with its first season in 1992, *Survivor*, the first network TV reality show, had a viewing audience greater than 50 million for the finale of the first season in 2000. Likewise, while fewer than fifty individuals kept online journals or diaries in 1996, according to writer Simon Firth, in the following decade free online journaling and blogging services like Open Diary, Live Journal, Blogger, and My Space had exploded. As Lupsa writes in the *Christian Science Monitor* in 2007, "Self-revelation is no longer the stuff of memoir, but a central feature in magazines, popular radio shows, traveling stage shows, websites, and more."

Although the campaign for more media access to courtrooms can be readily placed into a larger cultural context, what is not apparent is whether it is a *cause* or an *effect* of the larger shift in American culture. As Lithwick says of the popularity of the O.J. Simpson trial, "It's not at all clear that television caused the madness that became O.J.-mania, or merely exposed it." Did the televising of the Simpson trial lead to a more media-hungry America, or had American culture already made the shift, and Court TV merely gave its citizens what they wanted? And finally, is it necessarily one or the other?

Questions such as these, that explore the root of the change, tend to frame it in negative terms. Many cite the push for cameras in courtrooms as demonstrative of a sensationalistic shift in the mainstream media. In an article in the *American Journalism Review*, Kevin Brass notes that to some journalists, "the 'must cover' attitude toward celebrity trials is another sign of the skewing of news judgment in broadcast journalism." Even outside of celebrity trials, many who resist the media's presence in courtrooms say that allowing the media to move into territory previously considered private, or sacred, like courtrooms, would be the first step down a slippery slope, both legally and culturally.

Others, however, don't see the shift as necessarily negative, and some even see it as decidedly positive. Perhaps, they say, America is becoming more honest, more transparent, and less secretive. In this light, allowing cameras into courtrooms signals a move toward a greater democracy, one where all branches of the government—including the judiciary—are accountable to the people. Tompkins writes, "The banning of cameras from the courtroom serves only one purpose. It preserves the mystique and mystery of the court but does nothing to illuminate the citizens. That is antithetical to democracy."

The debate over cameras in courtrooms ultimately gets at larger questions about American society. To what extent is a public trial public? Does the defendant's right to a fair trial trump the public's right of access? To whom does the American courtroom belong—to the judges who preside over it, or to the citizens? Does the recording or televising of a proceeding trivialize the judicial process? These are among the questions that are addressed in *At Issue: Should Cameras Be Allowed in Courtrooms?*

1

Cameras Should Be Allowed in Courtrooms

Barbara Cochran

Barbara Cochran is president of the Radio-Television News Directors Association (RTNDA), the world's largest professional organization of electronic journalists.

Recently proposed legislation that would grant electronic media access to federal court proceedings should be passed, as it would allow the public to see what goes on in federal courtrooms. Public access to judicial proceedings is a right guaranteed by the First Amendment. Giving the American people a firsthand look at what takes place in the nation's courtrooms will result in a citizenry better informed about the decisions that affect their lives. For example, it was shown that Americans knew more about the Supreme Court after portions of the 2000 presidential election dispute proceedings were aired. When electronic media are prohibited from the courtroom, citizens are dependent on the reportage of journalists—which can be inaccurate—rather than witnessing the events themselves and drawing their own conclusions. Critics of electronic media in courtrooms fear potential disruptions, as well as adverse effects on witnesses and jurors. But a pilot program that ran during the early 1990s showed that these concerns were unfounded. Radio and television coverage of federal courts should be allowed except when a harmful effect of such coverage can be demonstrated.

Barbara Cochran, Testimony before the United States Senate Committee on the Judiciary, "Cameras in the Courtroom," Washington, D.C., 2005. Reproduced by permission of the author.

Under present law, radio and television coverage of federal criminal and civil proceedings at both the trial and appellate levels is effectively banned. The Sunshine in the Courtroom Act of 2005 represents an important step toward removing the cloak of secrecy surrounding our judicial system by giving all federal judges the discretion to allow cameras in their courts under a three-year pilot program. Similarly, legislation introduced by Chairman [Arlen] Specter would open our nation's highest court to audiovisual coverage and would instill a sense of public trust in our judicial process by allowing Americans to witness for themselves what transpires within the United States Supreme Court, thus gaining insight into decisions that affect their daily lives.

It is simply not right that Americans form their opinions about how our judicial system functions based on what they see and hear on the latest episode of *Judge Judy* or *CSI*, entertaining as those television programs may be. Nor does it make sense that the nominees for the Supreme Court are widely seen in televised hearings conducted by this Committee [the Senate Committee on the Judiciary], only to disappear from public view the moment they are sworn in as justices.

RTNDA's [Radio-Television News Directors Association's] members are the people who have demonstrated that television and radio coverage works at the state and local level, and they can make it work on the federal level. RTNDA strongly believes that permitting electronic coverage of federal judicial proceedings—from federal district courts to the United States Supreme Court—is the right thing to do as a matter of sound public policy. Moreover, RTNDA believes that the decision to allow cameras in federal courtrooms is a legislative prerogative. Passage of this legislation will send a message to judges that giving the public access to courts through televised proceedings is a right and an opportunity, not an inconvenience.

A Public Forum

RTNDA respectfully submits that there is no compelling reason not to support the passage of this legislation. The First

Amendment fight of the public to attend trials has been upheld by [the] U.S. Supreme Court. The presence of cameras in many state courtrooms is routine and well-accepted. The anachronistic, blanket ban on electronic media coverage of federal proceedings conflicts with the values of open judicial proceedings and disserves the people. A courtroom is, by nature, a public forum where citizens have the right to be present, and where their presence historically has been thought to enhance the integrity and quality of what takes place.

The potential for disruption to judicial proceedings [by electronic media] has been minimized.

The interests of our citizens are not fully served, in this day and age, by opening federal courtrooms to a limited number of observers, including the press, who can publicize any irregularities they note. In practice, what goes on inside a courtroom can only be effectively reported if the court permits journalists to use the best technology for doing so. There is no principled basis for allowing the print media and not the electronic media to use the tools of their trade inside federal courtrooms. Only the electronic media can serve the function of allowing interested members of the public not privileged to be in the courtroom to see and hear for themselves what occurs. As Judge Nancy Gertner aptly stated in testimony before this body's Subcommittee on Administrative Oversight and the Courts [in 2000], "public proceedings in the twenty-first century necessarily mean televised proceedings."

Electronic Media Is Unobtrusive

Technological advances in recent decades have been extraordinary, and the potential for disruption to judicial proceedings has been minimized. The cameras available today are small, unobtrusive, and designed to operate without additional light. Moreover, the electronic media can be required to "pool" their coverage in order to limit the equipment and personnel present in the courtroom, further minimizing disruption.

It cannot seriously be disputed that audiovisual coverage, which would allow for complete and direct observation of the demeanor, tone, credibility, contentiousness, and perhaps even the competency and veracity of the participants, is the best means through which to advance the public's right to know as it pertains to the actions of the federal judiciary. Public access to judicial proceedings should not and need not be limited to reading second-hand accounts in newspapers, or hearing them on radio or seeing them on television. By nature, the electronic media is uniquely suited to ensure that the maximum number of citizens have direct and unmediated access to important events.

Admittedly, the electronic media is not a foreign element in the coverage of federal courts. Since the O.J. Simpson murder trial [of 1995, in which Simpson was tried and acquitted for killing his ex-wife and her friend], many have been quick to point the finger at the camera as the cause of "sensationalism" and public distaste for our legal process. The empirical evidence to the contrary is overwhelming—the camera shows what happens; it is not a cause. Moreover, the prohibition on audiovisual coverage of federal judicial proceedings has resulted in viewers witnessing those events that take place on the courthouse steps, not those transpiring where it matters most—inside the courtroom.

More Benefits than Adverse Effects

Jurors, prosecutors, lawyers, witnesses and judges on both the state and federal levels have overwhelmingly reported for the last decade or so that the unobtrusive camera has not had an adverse impact on trials or appellate proceedings. The pilot cameras program conducted by six federal districts and the Second and Ninth Circuit Courts of Appeals between 1991 and 1993 was a resounding success, resulting in a recommendation that cameras be allowed in all federal courts. All 50 states now permit some manner of audiovisual coverage of court proceedings. The District of Columbia is the only jurisdiction that prohibits trial and appellate coverage entirely. 43 states allow electronic coverage at the trial level.

Comprehensive studies conducted in 28 states show that television coverage of court proceedings has significant social and educational benefits. Most conclude that a silent, unobtrusive in-court camera provides the public with more and better information about, and insight into, the functioning of the courts. Many have found that the presence of cameras does not impede the fair administration of justice, does not compromise the dignity of the court, and does not impair the orderly conduct of judicial proceedings. In the hundreds of thousands of judicial proceedings covered electronically across the country since 1981, to the best of RTNDA's knowledge there has not been a single case where the presence of a courtroom camera has resulted in a verdict being overturned, or where a camera was found to have any effect whatsoever on the ultimate result.

Simultaneous audiovisual coverage of judicial proceedings improves the media's overall ability to accurately report on them.

It is also worth noting that simultaneous audiovisual coverage of judicial proceedings improves the media's overall ability to accurately report on them. Such coverage affords a greater pool of reporters instantaneous access. In-court events, including quotations, can be verified simply by playing back an audio or videotape. As one New York study found, "reporting on court proceedings, both by newspaper and broadcast reporters, frequently is more accurate and comprehensive when cameras are present."

2000 Election Dispute

One compelling illustration of the public benefits resulting from audiovisual coverage of judicial proceedings involves the presidential election dispute in the fall of 2000. Given Florida state rules that permit cameras in the courtroom, the nation was able to watch and listen live as the Florida courts, including the state's Supreme Court, heard arguments in President [George W.] Bush's bid to throw out hand-counted ballots that former Vice President Al Gore hoped would win him the presidency.

In response to requests from numerous media organizations, including RTNDA, to allow television coverage of the subsequent oral arguments before the United States Supreme Court, Chief Justice [William] Rehnquist wrote, "the Court recognizes the intense public interest in the case and for that reason today has decided to release a copy of the audiotape of the argument promptly after the conclusion of the argument." Radio stations played the tapes in their entirety; their television counterparts played long excerpts, supplemented with photos and the familiar artists' sketches. Later, Chief Justice Rehnquist told a CNN reporter that he was very pleased with the reception that the playing of the court's audiotapes had gotten. People who before the election couldn't have named one justice now could name all nine. As divisive as the 2000 electoral contest was, the openness of the courtrooms produced the common understanding and acceptance necessary for political closure.

The Supreme Court has released audiotapes of other high profile cases in recent years, thus permitting the public to hear oral argument concerning such serious issues as United States courts' jurisdiction over claims by foreign citizens held at the Guantanamo Naval Base and whether the government may withhold constitutional protections from a U.S. citizen detained as an "enemy combatant." While the electronic media has welcomed release of these select recordings, they are no substitute for consistent, complete audiovisual coverage. Significantly, in response to questions posed by members of this Committee during his confirmation hearings, our new Chief Justice, John Roberts, stated that he is open to the idea of televising Supreme Court proceedings.

The time has come for Congress to legislate.

Eyewitness Opportunity

Indeed, because of the federal ban, American citizens have been deprived of the benefits of first-hand coverage of significant issues that have come before the United States federal district courts, federal appellate courts, and the Supreme Court in recent years, For example:

- Whether the government can take possession of a person's private property and transfer it to developers to encourage economic development;

- Whether executing juveniles constitutes cruel and unusual punishment;

- Whether the term "Under God" in the Pledge of Allegiance is unconstitutional;

- Whether a state university may consider race and ethnicity in its admissions process;

- Whether parents have a constitutionally protected right to prevent schools from providing information on sexual topics to their children.

In contrast, on October 19 [2005], people throughout the world were able to turn on their television sets (or their computers) to witness for themselves opening proceedings in the trial of [Iraqi president] Saddam Hussein and seven of his associates accused of crimes against humanity. The judges involved and the Iraqi people apparently understood how critically important it was to make this process truly public. Ironically, if the United States had successfully argued to have the case come before one of our federal courts, our laws would have prohibited broadcast of the trial.

For whatever reasons, federal courts have not, on their own motion, taken steps to permit electronic coverage of their proceedings. Therefore, RTNDA respectfully submits that the time has come for Congress to legislate. As federal district Judge Leonie Brinkema wrote in rejecting requests for televised coverage of the trial of alleged terrorist Zacarias Moussaoui, whether or not to permit cameras in federal courtrooms is a question of social and political policy best left to the United States Congress. The legislation proposed by Senators [Chuck] Grassley and [Charles] Schumer represents a careful approach by giving federal judges at both the trial and appellate levels the discretion to allow cameras in their courts under a three-year pilot program. At its conclusion, Congress and federal judges would be given an opportunity to review the program. Similarly, Chairman Specter's bill would afford a majority of the justices the discretion to disallow coverage where they believe the due process rights of a party would be violated.

The public has a right to see how justice is carried out in our nation.

Allow Access with Exceptions

I should mention here that RTNDA believes that federal law governing television coverage of the judicial branch should be grounded in a presumption that such coverage will be allowed unless it can be demonstrated that it would have a unique, adverse effect on the pursuit of justice or prejudice the rights of the parties in any particular case. Placing decisions as to whether or not to "pull the plug" on electronic coverage in the hands of the parties would render the legislation ineffective.

The public has a right to see how justice is carried out in our nation. As the Supreme Court has stated, people in an open society do not demand infallibility from their institutions, but it will be difficult for them to accept what they are prohibited from observing. Public scrutiny will help reform our legal system, dispel myth and rumors that spread as a result of ignorance, and strengthen the ties between citizens and their government. The courtroom camera not only gets the story right, it creates a record of the proceedings and opens a limited space to a broader audience. Experience shows that cameras in the courtroom work and that they do not interfere with administration or infringe on the rights of defendants or witnesses. RTNDA members have covered hundreds if not thousands of state proceedings across the country without incident and with complete respect for the integrity of the judicial process.

In the same way the public's right to know has been significantly enhanced by the presence of cameras in the House and then the Senate over the past two decades, the proposed legislation that is the subject of today's hearing has the potential to illuminate our federal courtrooms, demystify an often intimidating legal system, and subject the federal judicial process to an appropriate level of public scrutiny. While both print and electronic media fulfill the important role of acting as a surrogate for the public, only television has the ability to provide the public with a close visual and aural approximation of actually witnessing events without physical attendance. It is time to provide unlimited seating to the workings of justice everywhere in the United States by permitting audiovisual coverage of federal judicial proceedings at all levels, including those before the United States Supreme Court.

2

Cameras Should Not Be Allowed in Courtrooms

Jan E. DuBois

Jan E. DuBois has been a U.S. district court judge for the Eastern District of Pennsylvania since 1988.

A pilot program that allowed electronic media access to proceedings in certain federal courts from 1991 to 1994 included the U.S. District Court for the Eastern District of Pennsylvania. The Federal Judicial Center evaluated the program and published a report in 1994 based on participating judges' ratings of the effects of cameras on their courtrooms. These judges' evaluations were both positive and negative, but among the more disturbing effects were several factors that affected witness testimony. Most judges who participated in the pilot program were not wholly opposed to cameras in the courtroom, but they were generally concerned about the impact the cameras would have on the parties, witnesses, and jurors. They emphasized the importance of retaining the authority to prohibit or limit the use of cameras in certain cases and expressed concerns that the media would only televise excerpts of a proceeding. Overall, the disadvantages of allowing cameras in the courtrooms are far greater than the advantages.

My statement will cover the pilot program providing for electronic media coverage of civil proceedings in selected federal trial and appellate courts, including my trial court, from July 1, 1991, to December 31, 1994. The pilot

Jan E. DuBois, Testimony before the United States Senate Committee on the Judiciary, "Cameras in the Courtroom," November 9, 2005.

courts for that program were, in addition to my court, the U.S. district courts for the Southern District of Indiana, District of Massachusetts, Eastern District of Michigan, Southern District of New York, Western District of Washington; and the U.S. courts of appeals for the second and ninth circuit. Those pilot courts were selected from courts that had volunteered to participate in the experiment. Selection criteria included size, civil case load, proximity to major metropolitan markets, and regional and circuit representation.

The pilot program authorized coverage only of civil proceedings. Guidelines were adopted by Judicial Conference. . . . The guidelines required reasonable advance notice of a request to cover a proceeding; prohibited photographing of jurors in the courtroom, in the jury deliberation room, or during recesses; allowed only one television camera and one still camera in trial courts and two television cameras and one still camera in appellate courts; and required the media to establish "pooling" arrangements when more than one media organization wanted to cover a proceeding. The guidelines also provided that the presiding judge had discretion to refuse, terminate or limit media coverage.

From July 1, 1991, through June 30, 1993, media organizations applied to cover a total of 257 cases in all of the pilot courts. Of these, 186 or 72% of the applications were approved, 42 or 16% were disapproved and the remainder were not acted on. Of the total of 257 cases in which applications were made, 78 were submitted in the Eastern District of Pennsylvania. Of the 78, 54 or 69% were approved, and the remainder were disapproved or not ruled on.

Details of the Pilot Program

The Eastern District of Pennsylvania had the greatest application and coverage activity. The federal judicial center report on the program attributed that result, at least in part, to the fact that it was the Second Largest District Court in the pilot program and had a very active media coordinator.

Of the 186 cases approved for coverage, 147 were actually recorded or photographed. Nineteen of the remaining 39 approved cases were either settled or otherwise terminated, and nine applications were withdrawn. In 11 cases, the media failed to appear.

The Eastern District of Pennsylvania, in a study undertaken at the completion of the pilot program on December 31, 1994, reported a total of 117 broadcasting requests from the media, 86 or 74% of which were approved, 16 or 14% of which were disapproved, and 15 of which were in cases that were settled. The breakdown of the 117 cases in which applications were approved discloses that almost half, 57 or 49%, were in the civil rights cases. Of the 57 civil rights cases in which applications were made, 42 or 74% were approved, and 15 or 12% were disapproved. Next in terms of percentage of requests were tort cases, 21 or 18%.

The Federal Judicial Center evaluated the pilot program and in 1994 published a report entitled *Electronic Media Coverage of Federal Civil Proceedings: An Evaluation of the Pilot Program in Six District Courts and Two Courts of Appeals*; Federal Judicial Center, 1994 ("Federal Judicial Center Report"). That report included ratings of effects of cameras in the courtroom by district judges who participated in the program. . . .

[Forty-six]% of the judges believed that, at least to some extent, cameras made witnesses less willing to appear in court.

The Program's Outcome

The ratings by the judges who participated in the program were both favorable and unfavorable. For me, the most disturbing ratings are these:

- 64% of the participating judges reported that, at least to some extent, cameras made witnesses more nervous.

- 46% of the judges believed that, at least to some extent, cameras made witnesses less willing to appear in court.

- 41% of the judges found that, at least to some extent, cameras distracted witnesses.

- 56% of the participating judges found that, at least to some extent, cameras violated witnesses' privacy.

The Federal Judicial Center report recommended that the Judicial Conference "authorize federal courts of appeals and district courts nationwide to provide camera access to civil proceedings in their courtrooms. . . ." Those recommendations were reviewed and approved by the Judicial Center staff, but were not reviewed by its board. As you know, the Judicial Conference disagreed with the conclusions drawn by the Federal Judicial Center report and barred cameras in district courts because of the potentially intimidating effect of cameras on parties, witnesses and jurors.

Before granting or denying an application for television coverage in cases before me in the pilot program, it was my practice to convene a conference or to address the matter at the final pretrial conference. The most commonly advanced objections during such conferences were these:

Adverse effect on parties. In some cases plaintiffs were concerned about disclosing matters of an extremely private nature such as family relationships, medical information, and financial information. Defendants expressed concern about the risks of damaging accusations made in a televised trial. In at least one case, a defense attorney said the threat of a televised trial would cause the defendant to consider settlement regardless of the merits of the case for the sole purpose of avoiding the television coverage.

Adverse effect on witnesses. Counsel were concerned that cameras would make witnesses less willing to appear and, when in court, would make witnesses more nervous. That presents a real concern for a trial judge. As a result, I was prepared to direct that the television camera be removed from the courtroom or not be operational during the testimony of any witness who objected to the camera.

My Personal Experience

I approved requests for television coverage in 3 cases—a product liability case on the first day of the program, July 1, 1991, a class action on behalf of all state prisoners in Pennsylvania in which prison conditions were challenged as unconstitutional, and a case filed by a Republican congressman against a Democratic lieutenant governor over the failure to call a special election at an early date for the congressman's vacated state senate seat. There were cameras in the courtroom for one day of the product liability case. There is no record of cameras in the courtroom in the two other cases.

In the one case in which cameras were present in my courtroom, the product liability case, there were no objections to the television coverage either from the parties or from witnesses. I did not allow cameras in the courtroom during jury selection. After the jury was convened, I asked whether any jurors had any objection to cameras in the courtroom with the *proviso* that the cameras would not focus on them. They had no objections.

I was also concerned during the product liability trial the camera would be in the courtroom on one day and then be removed, and that is exactly what happened—the camera was in the courtroom only one day. Anticipating that potential problem, I told the jurors that there was no guarantee that the media would televise the entire trial and that it might be "here today and gone tomorrow." I also instructed them that they were not to conclude that evidence or argument presented during a time when a camera was in the courtroom was any more or less important than any other part of the trial.

Judges' Concerns

Overall, the views of my colleagues who participated in the cameras in the courtroom pilot were not unfavorable. However, most of the judges who commented were concerned about the adverse impact of cameras in the courtroom on parties, witnesses and jurors and deemed it of critical importance to retain the authority to disapprove of use of cameras, particularly in high profile cases, and to limit the use of cameras in cases such as by not televising the testimony of a witness who objected and not focusing on jurors. Some judges who participated in the program were also concerned that the media would not be interested in televising an entire proceeding, and would use only short segments of a proceeding with voice-overs. I am not going to comment on the educational benefit of televising a small portion of a trial except to say that it would be very difficult to provide much valuable information about the judicial system in that type of presentation.

At the trial level, the disadvantages of cameras in the courtroom far outweigh the advantages.

My personal view is that, at the trial level, the disadvantages of cameras in the courtroom far outweigh the advantages. In such a setting, the camera is likely to do more than report the proceeding—it is likely to influence the substance of the proceeding. I say that because of the concerns I have expressed regarding objections of parties to televised proceedings and the potential impact of a television camera on witnesses and jurors.

The paramount responsibility of a district judge is to uphold the Constitution, which guarantees citizens the right to a fair and impartial trial. In my opinion, cameras in the district court could seriously jeopardize that right.

3

Cameras Should Be Allowed in Criminal Trials with Consent of All Parties

Barbara E. Bergman

Barbara E. Bergman served as president of the National Association of Criminal Defense Lawyers and is a professor of law at the University of New Mexico School of Law.

The issue of camera access to courtrooms is not merely a matter of the media's or the public's right of access. In criminal cases, these rights must be weighed against the accused's Sixth Amendment right to a fair trial. As it is currently written, Senate bill S. 829 (the Sunshine in the Courtroom Act of 2005) does not sufficiently balance these rights. The National Association of Criminal Defense Lawyers (NACDL) would like to see the bill amended so that cameras are only allowed in district court criminal proceedings when all parties consent. The NACDL generally supports the expanded use of cameras in courtrooms as a means of providing the public with a greater understanding of the judicial process and holding the participants to a higher level of accountability. But there is also substantial reason to believe that the presence of cameras in courtrooms may influence the behavior of participants, and ultimately threaten the defendant's right to a fair trial.

Barbara E. Bergman, National Association of Criminal Defense Lawyers, testimony before the United States Senate Committee on the Judiciary, "Cameras in the Courtroom," November 9, 2005.

While current rules do not permit cameras in federal district courts, the NACDL's members have experience with televised proceedings in their state courts and the two camera-accessible federal appellate courts. Indeed, the NACDL's immediate past president, Barry Scheck, served as defense counsel in the most hotly debated example of extended media coverage [the 1995 O.J. Simpson murder trial]. Before explaining the NACDL's position regarding this issue, I am compelled to make two preliminary disclosures. First, in discussing this issue with our Board of Directors recently, it was apparent that there is no consensus within the defense community regarding the overall desirability of cameras in courtrooms. The position of our association reflects that diversity of experience and opinion. Second, in keeping with the NACDL's mission, our position is limited to criminal proceedings, which are subject to both broader constitutional guarantees and, generally speaking, broader public interest.

The question of whether cameras should be permitted in the federal courts cannot be answered merely by invoking the media's or public's "right of access." The Supreme Court has held that there is no constitutional right of access for cameras in the courtroom: The decision to ban cameras is simply a restriction on the manner of the media's access to trials, and it is rationally based. In criminal cases, the purported value of televised court proceedings must be weighed against the accused's constitutional rights to due process and a fair trial. The NACDL believes that [Senate bill] S. 829 does not strike the right balance. We would like to see the bill amended so as to authorize cameras in district court criminal proceedings and interlocutory appeals only with the express consent of the parties. In all other criminal matters coming before the United States Courts of Appeals and the Supreme Court, the NACDL favors access for cameras.

Arguments in Favor of Cameras in Court

To the extent that cameras in the courtroom promote greater public understanding of the judicial process and the constitutional protections that apply to that process, we generally support their expanded use. A citizenry that understands such fundamental guarantees as the presumption of innocence, the government's burden to prove the offense elements beyond a reasonable doubt, and the accused's Fifth Amendment right to remain silent will more faithfully fulfill the solemn duties of jury service. Beyond this positive effect on potential jurors, extended media coverage of criminal trials may foster respect for outcomes that do not necessarily comport with public sentiment. In some cases, televised trials may dispel the damning stigma of pretrial publicity and help to restore the reputation of a criminal defendant against whom charges are dismissed or a not guilty verdict is returned. Finally, televised trials may provide the public with greater insight regarding the appropriateness of certain laws and the potential need for reform. Court TV must be credited for its considerable contributions in all of these areas.

However, these societal benefits are largely intuitive and difficult to measure. Of greater concern to the NACDL are the values underlying the defendant's Sixth Amendment right to a public trial. The purposes of this guarantee are to protect the accused from the abuses that may attend secret proceedings and to subject courtroom events to public scrutiny. Aside from deterring official misconduct, the print and broadcast media make an invaluable contribution to our justice system by shining a light on miscarriages of justice when they do occur. The instances where cameras have helped to prevent or expose injustice are too numerous to mention, and this factor should weigh heavily in any policy decision regarding courtroom access.

Not unrelated is the notion that televised trials encourage greater preparation and a higher standard of professionalism. It stands to reason that some lawyers and judges—aware that their actions will be televised—will strive to perform at a higher level and comport themselves with a greater degree of civility and ethics. If true, this may enhance both the quality of our justice system and public perceptions of the legal profession. This factor, therefore, tends to bolster the foregoing arguments in favor of cameras in the courtroom.

The presence of cameras . . . may cause lawyers, judges, jurors, defendants and witnesses to act differently.

Arguments Against Cameras in Court

One primary concern regarding cameras in the courtroom is that they will affect the participants' behavior in ways that would undermine the fair administration of justice. That is, the presence of cameras and the attendant glare of publicity may cause lawyers, judges, jurors, defendants and witnesses to act differently and to base their decisions on irrelevant factors. In rare cases, the prejudicial impact may be apparent, providing grounds for relief, but more often the effect will be "so subtle as to defy detection by the accused or control by the judge" [as written in the *Estes v. Texas* decision of 1965].

If jurors are filmed and their verdict publicized, concern about how their verdict will be accepted by the mass television audience may invade the deliberations process. The decision to televise a trial signals to the jury that the case is celebrated or notorious and that their verdict is to be scrutinized by the viewing public. Defendants are less likely to receive a fair trial when jurors feel the need to reconcile their verdict with strong public sentiments in favor of a particular result. As U.S. District Court Judge Edward F. Harrington said:

> I am disinclined to allow cameras into the courtroom because it lets jurors know this is an unusual, that is, a celebrated case. And when jurors are asked to make a judgment in an ordinary case, that is a heavy responsibility. When they are asked to make a judgment in a celebrated case, I think that puts undue pressure on them. And it might distort the verdict.

There is some evidence that citizens will be less willing to serve on juries if there are cameras in the courtroom. Should a case result in a mistrial, past television coverage may make it more difficult to select an impartial jury for the retrial.

Effects on Judges, Witnesses, and Defendants

While life-tenured federal judges enjoy a greater degree of insulation from public and political pressure than their elected counterparts, this is still an area of concern. Like other participants, judges may tailor their actions to win the admiration or approval of the viewing public and commentators. Even the appearance of this can undermine confidence in the justice system and the fairness of the proceeding, because [as law professor David A. Harris wrote] "judges as the embodiment of the process, must appear above reproach at all times if the system and the rule of law are to receive respect."

Televised proceedings can adversely affect witness behavior in many ways. The prospect of television coverage may chill witness cooperation and heighten the reluctance of some witnesses to appear and testify. Not just an issue for the prosecution, the effect of cameras in deterring witnesses from testifying may have serious implications for a defendant's right to receive a fair trial. Just as damaging to the truth-seeking process, some witnesses may exaggerate or distort their testimony so as to gain personal publicity. The effect of television coverage may also impact witness demeanor—for example, making self-conscious witnesses appear agitated or ill-tempered—thus hindering the jury's vital efforts to determine credibility. Provisions in S. 829 that would permit the witness the option of obscuring their face and voice would not fully address such concerns, given that the witness's name and other personal facts would be televised.

In addition to these potential threats to the defendant's right to a fair trial, courtroom cameras may alter the defendant's behavior as well. As with witnesses, cameras in the courtroom may affect the accused's demeanor and willingness to testify. More fundamentally, the prospect of extended media coverage may discourage the accused from exercising their right to trial in the first place. This may be of particular concern in cases involving notorious, repugnant or humiliating accusations or corporate defendants unwilling to expose themselves to negative publicity. Even when the accused is acquitted, the stain on their reputation is not easily erased, and camera coverage may exacerbate this unwarranted punishment. Televised trials also may subject the accused (or other participants) to harassment of physical threats during the course of the trial, necessitating additional security measures at public expense.

The consent of the parties . . . should be required before cameras are permitted.

Striking the Right Balance

The sponsors of S. 829 have wisely avoided a role authorizing unrestricted camera access. Rather than placing the ultimate decision in the hands of the presiding judge, however, we think the consent of the parties—the accused (acting with the advice of counsel) and the government—should be required before cameras are permitted to televise criminal trials or interlocutory appeals. The positive or negative effects of cameras depend on the facts and circumstances of each case. The parties, who are familiar with the witnesses who will testify, the evidence that will be offered, and other facts that might indicate the potential for prejudice, are in the best position to determine the appropriateness of cameras.

Moreover, permitting the parties to withhold their consent avoids the time-consuming distraction of litigation regarding the judge's decision to permit or forbid camera coverage. The decision to bring cameras into the courtroom is usually made a few days prior to the start of trial. The defendant, if he opposes camera coverage, would be required to enter into an extended process of brief writing and oral argument to convince the trial judge that cameras will unfairly prejudice his client. Often, you will have a criminal defense attorney who is a solo practitioner or works out of a small firm and a defendant who has severely limited financial resources to pay for his defense; other times, the defendant will be represented by an attorney appointed under the Criminal Justice Act or employed by one of the Federal or Community Public Defenders. Forcing a defense attorney to focus on such matters at a critical moment in a case and requiring a defendant or taxpayers to pay for that representation on an issue that is irrelevant to a determination of guilt or innocence undermines the "proposition that the criminal trial under our Constitution has a clearly defined purpose, to provide a fair and reliable determination of guilt, and no procedure or occurrence which seriously threatens to divert it from that purpose can be tolerated" [*Estes v. Texas*].

This position is supported by the fact that any prejudice as a result of the decision to allow cameras will be difficult to detect and virtually impossible to rectify. "The prejudices of television may be so subtle that it escapes the ordinary methods of proof" [*Estes v. Texas*]. Any rule that fails to honor the accused's objection would too easily jeopardize the fundamental right to a fair trial, upon which the accused's life or liberty depends, for the sake of less important societal goals. While we support efforts to ensure more sunshine on our democratic institutions, that goal should not be allowed to eclipse the fundamental purpose of a criminal trial: not education, not entertainment, but justice.

4

Cameras Should Be Allowed in the Supreme Court

Arlen Specter

Arlen Specter is a Republican senator from Pennsylvania serving his fifth term. He is a ranking member of the Senate Judiciary Committee.

If passed, Senate bill S. 344 would require U.S. Supreme Court proceedings to be televised except in cases where it is deemed harmful. This legislation would increase the public's awareness and understanding of how the nation's highest court works, which is essential considering the extent to which the Supreme Court's decisions affect Americans' daily lives. Just as C-SPAN covers congressional proceedings, giving Americans a firsthand look at how their government is being run, so should the Supreme Court allow the nation's citizens a look at how it makes its decisions. Some opponents of cameras in the Supreme Court have voiced concern that the exposure would bring notoriety to the justices. Yet several members of the Supreme Court have already appeared on various television programs. Furthermore, Justices John Paul Stevens, Stephen Breyer, Antonin Scalia, and Ruth Bader Ginsburg have indicated that they would support televising the Court's proceedings. While some wonder whether Congress has the authority to require the televising of the Supreme Court, there is substantial reason to assume that it does.

I have sought recognition to comment about S. 344, which provides for the televising of Supreme Court proceedings.

Arlen Specter, United States Senate floor speech on S. 344, January 29, 2007.

The essential provision is to require televising proceedings at the Supreme Court of the United States unless the Court determines on an individual basis that there would be an inappropriate occasion and a violation of the due process rights of the parties.

The thrust of this legislation is to bring public attention and understanding of how the Supreme Court of the United States functions, because it is the ultimate decisionmaker on so many—virtually all of the cutting edge questions of our day. The Supreme Court of the United States made the decision in *Bush v. Gore* [2000], essentially deciding who would be President of the United States. The Supreme Court decides cases on the death penalty, as to who will die.

It decides by 5-to-4 decisions so many vital cases, including partial-birth or late-term abortion, deciding who will live. It decides the question of who will be elected, controlling the constitutional decision on campaign contributions. It decides the constitutionality—again, and all of the cases I mentioned are 5 to 4—on school prayer, on school vouchers, on whether the Ten Commandments may be publicly displayed, on whether affirmative action will be permitted, on whether eminent domain will be allowed—the taking of private property for governmental purposes. The Supreme Court of the United States decides the power of the President as illustrated by *Hamdan v. Rumsfeld* [2006]—that the President does not have a blank check and that the President is not a monarch.

The Impact of the Supreme Court

The Supreme Court of the United States, again in a series of 5-to-4 decisions, has decided what is the power of Congress, declaring in *U.S. v. Morrison* [2000] the legislation to protect women against violence unconstitutional because the Court questioned our "method of reasoning," raising a fundamental question as to where is the superiority of the Court's method of reasoning over that of the Congress. But that kind of decision, simply stated, is not understood.

Or the Supreme Court of the United States dealing with the Americans With Disabilities Act, making two decisions which are indistinguishable, upholding the statute on a paraplegic crawling into the courthouse in Tennessee and striking down the constitutionality of the statute when dealing with employment discrimination. They did so on a manufactured test of congruence and proportionality, which is literally picked out of thin air.

Under our Constitution, I respect the standing of the Supreme Court of the United States to be the final arbiter and to make the final decisions. But it is, I think, fundamental that the Court's work, the Court's operation ought to be more broadly understood. That can be achieved by television. Just as these proceedings are televised on C-SPAN, just as the House of Representatives is televised on C-SPAN, so, too, could the Supreme Court be televised on an offer made by C-SPAN to have a separate channel for Supreme Court oral arguments. There are many opportunities for the Court to receive this kind of coverage, to inform the American people about what is going on so that the American people can participate in a meaningful way as to whether the Court is functioning as a super-legislature—which it ought not to do, that being entrusted to the Congress and State legislatures, with the Court's responsibility being to interpret the law.

A number of the Justices have stated support for televising the Supreme Court.

It should be noted that the individual Justices of the Supreme Court have already been extensively televised. Chief Justice [John G.] Roberts and Justice [John Paul] Stevens were on "Prime Time" on ABC TV. Justice Ruth Bader Ginsburg was on CBS with Mike Wallace. Justice [Stephen] Breyer was on "FOX News" Sunday. Justice [Antonin] Scalia and Justice Breyer had an extensive debate last December [2006], which is available for viewing on the Web—and in television archives. So there has been very extensive participation by Court members, which totally undercuts one of the arguments, that the notoriety would imperil the security of Supreme Court Justices.

Justices in Support

It is also worth noting that a number of the Justices have stated support for televising the Supreme Court. For example, Justice Stevens, in an article by Henry Weinstein on July 14, 1989, said he supported cameras in the Supreme Court and told the annual Ninth Circuit Judicial Conference at about the same time that, "In my view, it is worth a try."

Justice Stevens has been quoted recently stating his favorable disposition to televising the Supreme Court.

Justice Breyer, during his confirmation hearings in 1994, indicated support for televising Supreme Court proceedings. He has since equivocated, but has also noted that it would be a wonderful teaching device.

In a December 13, 2006, article by David Pereira, Justice Scalia said he favored cameras in the Supreme Court to show the public that a majority of the caseload involves dull stuff.

In December of 2000, an article by Marjorie Cohn noted Justice Ruth Bader Ginsburg's support of camera coverage, so long as it is gavel to gavel—which can be arranged.

Justice [Samuel] Alito, in his Senate confirmation hearings last year [2006], said that as a member of the Third Circuit Court of Appeals he voted to admit cameras.

He added that it would be presumptuous of him to state a final position until he had consulted with his colleagues, if confirmed. But at a minimum, he promised to keep an open mind, noting that he had favored television in the Third Circuit Court of Appeals.

Dissenting Justices

Justice [Anthony] Kennedy, according to a September 10, 1990, article by James Rubin, told a group of visiting high school students that cameras in the Court were "inevitable," as he put it. He has since equivocated, stating that if any of his colleagues raise serious objections, he would be reluctant to see the Supreme Court televised. Chief Justice Roberts said in his confirmation hearings that he would keep an open mind. Justice [Clarence] Thomas has opposed cameras. Justice David Souter has opposed televising the Supreme Court. Justice Souter has been the most outspoken opponent of televising the Supreme Court, saying if cameras rolled into the Supreme Court, they would roll over his—as he put it—over his dead body—a rather colorful statement. But there has been, as noted, considerable sentiment by quite a number of the Justices as to their personal views expressing favorable disposition toward televising the Supreme Court.

The question inevitably arises as to whether Congress has the authority to require televising Supreme Court proceedings, and I submit there is ample authority on Congress's generalized control over administrative matters in the Court. For example, it is the Congress which decides how many Justices there will be on the Court. It is remembered that President [Franklin D.] Roosevelt, in the mid to late 1930s, proposed a so-called "packing of the Court" plan to raise the number to 15. But that is a congressional judgment. The Congress decides when the Supreme Court will begin its term: on the first Monday of every October. The Congress decides what number will constitute a quorum of the Supreme Court: six. The Congress of the United States has instituted timelines that are required to be observed by the Supreme Court when determining timeliness in habeas corpus cases. So there is ample authority for the proposition that televising the Supreme Court would be constitutional.

The Bill's Constitutionality

There is an article [from] May 2007 by Associate Professor Bruce Peabody of the political science department of Fairleigh Dickinson University, and in that article, Professor Peabody makes a strong analysis that congressional action to televise the Supreme Court would be constitutional. Also, in that article Professor Peabody refers at length to the legislation which I introduced in 2005 and says that it would be constitutional and observes that: "A case could be made for reform giving rise to more wide-ranging and creative thinking of the role and status of the judiciary if the Supreme Court was, in fact, televised." He further notes that: "Televising the Supreme Court could stimulate a more general discussion about whether other reforms of the court might be in order." He notes that: "The so-called Specter bill would be meaningful in giving wider play to a set of conversations that have long been coursing through the academy about the relationship between the court and the Congress."

The electronic media, television, is the basic way of best informing the public about what the Supreme Court does.

The Supreme Court itself, in the 1980 decision in *Richmond Newspapers v. Virginia*, implicitly recognized, perhaps even sanctioned, televising the Court because in that case, the Supreme Court noted that a public trial belongs not only to the accused but to the public and the press as well; and that people acquire information on Court proceedings chiefly through the print and electronic media. But we know as a factual matter that the electronic media, television, is the basic way of best informing the public about what the Supreme Court does.

Interest in the 2000 Election Dispute

There was enormous public interest in the case of *Bush v. Gore* argued in the Supreme Court in December of 2000 after the challenge had been made to the calculation of the electoral votes from the State of Florida and whether the so-called chads suggested or showed that Vice President [Al] Gore was the rightful claimant for those electoral votes or whether then-Governor [George W.] Bush was the rightful claimant.

The streets in front of the Supreme Court chambers across the green from the Senate Chamber were filled with television trucks. At that time, Senator [Joseph] Biden and I wrote to Chief Justice [William] Rehnquist urging that the proceedings be televised and got back a prompt reply in the negative.

But at least on that day the Supreme Court did release an audiotape when the proceedings were over, and the Supreme Court has made available virtually contemporaneous audio tapes since. But I suggest the audio tapes do not fill the bill. They do not have the audience. They do not have the impact. They do not convey the forcefulness that televising the Supreme Court would.

There has been considerable commentary lately about the Court's workload and the Court's caseload. Chief Justice Roberts, for example, noted that the Justices: "Hear about half the number of cases they did 25 years ago." And, he remarked that from his vantage point, outside the Court: "They could contribute more to the clarity and uniformity of the law by taking more cases."

They have a very light backlog. In the 2005 term, only 87 cases were argued and 69 signed opinions were issued, which is a decrease from prior years. They have left many of the splits in the circuits undecided. Former Senator [Mike] DeWine, when serving on the Judiciary Committee, asked Justice Alito about the unresolved authority at the circuit level. Now

Justice Alito characterized that as "undesirable." But that happens because of the limited number of cases which the Supreme Court takes.

More Court Oversight

There has also been concern, as noted in an article by Stuart Taylor and Ben Wittes captioned, "Of Clerks and Perks," that the four clerks per Justice constitute an undesirable allocation of resources, and the Taylor-Wittes article cites the Justices' extensive extracurricular traveling, speaking, and writing, in addition to their summer recesses and the vastly reduced docket as evidence that something needs to be done to spur the Court into taking more cases.

If the Court were to be televised, there would be more focus on what the Court is doing.

If the Court were to be televised, there would be more focus on what the Court is doing. That focus can be given without television, but once the Supreme Court becomes the center of attraction, the center of attention, articles such as that written by Taylor and Wittes would have much more currency.

The commentators have also raised a question about the pooling of the applications for certiorari. There were, in the 2005 term, some 8,521 filers. Most of those are petitions for certiorari. That is the fancy Latin word for whether the Court will grant process to hear the case from the lower courts. As we see, the Court acts on a very small number of those cases. Only 87 cases were argued that year in a term when more than 8,500 filings were recorded, most of those constituting cases which could have been heard. And, the Supreme Court has adopted a practice of the so-called "cert pool," a process used by eight of the nine Justices. Only Justice Stevens maintains a practice of reviewing the cert petitions himself on an individual basis, of course, assisted by his clerks. But when the Court is charged with the responsibility of deciding which cases to hear, it is my view that it is very problematic and, in my judgment, inappropriate for the Justices not to be giving individualized attention, at least through their clerks, and not having a cert pool where eight of the Justices have delegated the job of deciding which cases are sufficiently important to hear to a pool.

Concern About Case Selection

We do not know the inner workings of the pool, but I believe it is fair and safe to infer that the judgments are made by clerks. Precisely what the level of reference and what the level of consultation with the Justices is we do not know, but when an application is made to the Supreme Court of the United States to hear a case, it is my view that there ought to be individualized consideration.

That also appeared to be the view of now Chief Justice John Roberts, who said in a 1997 speech, according to a September 20, 2000, article in the *Legal Times* by reporter Tony Mauro where then-private practitioner John Roberts said he "found the pool disquieting, in that it made clerks a bit too significant in determining the Court's docket."

Chief Justice William Howard Taft ... said that review and public scrutiny was the best way to keep the judges on their toes.

I would suggest that is an understatement, to give that kind of power to the clerks and, beyond that, to give that kind of power to the clerks in a pool, where the individual Justices do not even make the delegation to their own clerks with whatever review they would then utilize but make that a delegation to a cert pool.

Public Scrutiny Needed

There have been many scholarly statements about the desirability of having greater oversight on what happens in the Supreme Court. Chief Justice William Howard Taft, who was the 10th Supreme Court Chief Justice and the 27th President of the United States, said that review and public scrutiny was the best way to keep the judges on their toes. And Justice Felix Frankfurter said that he longed for the day when the Supreme Court would receive as much attention as the World Series because the status of the Supreme Court depended upon its reputation with the people.

These are the exact words of Chief Justice William Howard Taft: "Nothing tends more to render judges careful in their decision and anxiously solicitous to do exact justice than the consciousness that every act of theirs is subject to the intelligent scrutiny of their fellow men and to candid criticism."

Justice Felix Frankfurter's exact words were: If the news media would cover the Supreme Court as thoroughly as it did the World Series, it would be very important since "public confidence in the judiciary hinges on the public perception of it."

I respect the Supreme Court's . . . role as the final arbiter, but say that there ought to be an understanding by the public.

We have a continuing dialogue and a continuing discussion as to the role of the Supreme Court in our society. We have the cutting edge questions consistently coming to the Court. We have them deciding the issues of who will live, who will die, what will be the status of prayer in the schools, what will be the status of our election laws, and through the vagaries of due process of law and equal protection, there are many standards which the Court can adopt. . . .

Then we have the Supreme Court being the final arbiter on what happens on Executive power, what happens at Guantanamo [controversial U.S. Navy base in Cuba where prisoners of war are detained], what is the responsibility of the President of the United States on military commissions, what is the responsibility under the Geneva Conventions. Here again, I respect the Supreme Court's decisions, respect their role as the final arbiter, but say that there ought to be an understanding by the public. It may be that there will never be a case which has more impact on the working of Government than the decision as to whether the Florida electoral votes would be counted for George Bush or for Albert Gore in the famous case of *Bush v. Gore*.

A prior version of this legislation [S. 344] came out of committee last year [2006] on a bipartisan 12-to-6 vote. It has very substantial cosponsorship. I urge my colleagues to consider it carefully. I urge the distinguished majority leader to look for a spot to bring such legislation to the Senate.

There is companion legislation which Senator [Chuck] Grassley is offering which gives the courts—the Supreme Court, courts of appeals, trial courts—the discretion to have television. My legislation, S. 344, is more targeted. It has a requirement as to the Supreme Court televising its proceedings unless there is some due-process violation which is considered on a case-by-case basis.

5

Cameras Should Not Be Allowed in the Supreme Court

Christina B. Whitman

Christina B. Whitman is the Francis A. Allen Collegiate Professor of Law at the University of Michigan Law School and former law clerk to Justice Lewis F. Powell Jr. of the U.S. Supreme Court.

There are understandable reasons for televising U.S. Supreme Court arguments. It is reasonable for the American public to want to understand the thinking behind so many important decisions, and other governmental branches have allowed electronic media access, as have lower courts. Such access, however, would be misleading, as oral arguments would receive attention that is disproportionate to their significance. For many justices, oral arguments play an insignificant role in their decision making, and the remarks they make during such arguments may not be indicative of their actual stances. Televising the Court's oral arguments, may result in undue attention for those justices with the sharpest wit, leading to a misrepresentation of the Court. Furthermore, the Supreme Court is already more open than the executive and legislative branches, rendering the televising of its arguments unnecessary. Although there would be some benefits to televising the Court's proceedings, the potentially harmful results are far more numerous.

Christina B. Whitman, "Televising the Court: A Category Mistake," *Michigan Law Review First Impressions*, vol. 106, 2007, pp. 5–7. Copyright © 2007 by the Michigan Law Review Association. Reproduced by permission.

The idea of televising Supreme Court oral arguments is undeniably appealing. Consequently, it is not surprising that
reporters and politicians have been pressuring the Court to
take this step. The other branches have been media-friendly
for years, and Supreme Court arguments are already open to
the public. Why should those of us who neither reside in
Washington, D.C., nor have the time to attend Court proceedings be asked to depend on reporters for descriptions of the
event? Even lower courts permit cameras. There is an understandable hunger for anything that will help us understand
these nine individuals who have so much power—who can
even choose a President, or at least hasten his anointment. Are
the Justices refusing to reveal themselves because they prefer
mystery, because they do not want the public to realize that
the Court is a human institution after all? Whatever the
Justices' motives, televising the Court's arguments is a terrible
idea. It is both misleading and unnecessary. Misleading because it would only randomly tell us something useful about
the Court, and unnecessary because the Court is already more
open than the other branches.

Oral arguments and announcements of decisions are the
only moments of public performance in the work of the
Court, but they are more performance than work. Arguments
come in the middle of the Justices' consideration of a case—
after considerable reading, discussion, and thought, but before
more of the same. Individual Justices use arguments differently. Some Justices simply do not work out their thoughts
orally. The Justice with whom I am most familiar, Justice
Lewis F. Powell, Jr., preferred to communicate through memo-
randa—even with his clerks. He was an extremely successful
litigator, but also a Southern gentleman. Showing off his intel-
ligence, much less asking a snide question or making a cutting
remark, was just not his style. Conversely, other Justices enjoy
the give-and-take with each other and with the advocates for
the sake of the encounter alone. Their dialogue may or may

not focus on what really matters to their decision in a case. They might just be pouncing on a weak argument for the pure pleasure of the kill. Either way, every comment is already overanalyzed for a hint as to what is on the Justices' minds.

Televising Arguments Would Be Misleading

Oral arguments already receive too much of the wrong kind of attention because Court watchers enjoy the game of predicting outcomes, and arguments provide an occasion to justify a story or a comment on a blog. But this attention gives arguments a misleading importance. It is common to say that a lawyer cannot win a case by her oral argument, but that she can lose her case that way. This is as it should be. Ideally, we want effective advocates for both sides, but we should hope that the Justices can rise above a poor argument and reach a result that reflects judgment and justice despite the shortcomings of its advocate. Most arguments are lost not by embarrassing advocacy, but rather because a lawyer is not always able to avoid admitting under direct questioning to a weakness in his case that was concealed in his brief.

The availability of transcripts already promotes emphasis on the kinds of insights and ripostes that can be conveyed in soundbites.

I enjoy reading the argument transcripts, which are now available almost immediately, and I use them in my classes. But they are a treat rather than a meal. On television and radio, the availability of transcripts already promotes emphasis on the kinds of insights and ripostes that can be conveyed in soundbites. There are Justices whose performances lend themselves to soundbites, who have a quick and provocative wit, and these Justices inevitably attract the most attention. Although these qualities are not inconsistent with greatness, they are not the qualities that make a Justice great. Despite the fun, focusing on these qualities distracts us from less flashy indications of excellence.

Supreme Court Is Already Open

So, the televising of oral arguments is misleading. It is also unnecessary. The Court has always been an open institution on the matters that count. The judiciary, at least at the appellate level, has always been required to expose the reasons underlying its actions more than either of the other branches of government—through the discipline of writing published opinions. That is the process through which judges are publicly accountable, and it has no counterpart in the political branches. It is not easy to spot dishonest reasoning or evaluate quality of judgment as captured in opinions, but it is possible. It requires effort, and it is admittedly undemocratic in that it also requires expertise. But it is exactly the process of struggling with writing that gives the judiciary its unique character and disciplines the tendency to rely on first impressions or subjective reactions. The voices of individual Justices can be traced through their separate opinions and even found in their collegial opinions for a group. But the individual is not obscured just to create an insiders' guessing game. The collegial process is the whole point. A Justice who speaks for the greatest number of her colleagues speaks with the most authority.

Is it naive to take the collegial character of the Court and its written opinions so seriously? Perhaps Justices delegate all this effort to their law clerks and are not really subject to the discipline of forming the written work. Perhaps they are only really engaged while on the bench, if there. To the extent that has happened, it is a betrayal of their obligation as Justices, a rejection of the key justification for judicial review—and certainly not something to be accepted or encouraged by over-emphasizing oral argument.

Changing the Court for the Worse

The standard arguments against televising the Court are true, too. Media attention might already be encouraging individual Justices to play to an audience. It would be unfortunate and inappropriate if the most attractive, or even the fastest wit, were to become the public face of the Court.

Let us not give verbal skill more importance than it deserves.

Politicians are accustomed to performing in the spotlight. They may not appreciate how invasive the camera can seem to people who have not lived their lives this way. Justice Powell took media access seriously, but he saw it as a duty rather than a pleasure. Even more exposure to public scrutiny might have made his years on the Court deeply uncomfortable. For people like Powell, for whom public service is an obligation and public performance a necessary evil, becoming a media celebrity might be too costly. Yet we need people like Justice Powell in part because they understand the costs of public scrutiny and the value of privacy.

A narrow view of accountability, one that reduces it to public observation, has already turned too much governmental decision-making away from substance. Media attention already focuses on the sharpest tongue on the bench. Let us not give verbal skill more importance than it deserves, lest it change the character of our least democratic but most open branch.

6

Supreme Court Proceedings Should Be Recorded but Not Televised

Scott C. Wilcox

While a student at the University of Michigan Law School, Scott C. Wilcox served as an executive editor of First Impressions, *the online journal of the* Michigan Law Review. *He is the author of* Local and State Campaign Management.

Several Supreme Court justices have indicated their opposition to allowing cameras in the Court, but close examination of their remarks reveals that they are actually opposed to televising Court proceedings, not to cameras themselves. Therefore, a reasonable compromise would be to video-record the proceedings and make this footage available for viewing, but not copying, at the National Archives. Admittedly, this solution may not satisfy advocates of electronic media access to the Court. They may argue that the National Archives is much less accessible to most Americans than television. However, televised coverage of the Court would most likely only air for a few days or weeks after the recording, while footage could be available in the National Archives indefinitely. Archived recordings of Supreme Court proceedings would also benefit historians, legal practitioners, scholars, and law students. Perhaps at some point the Supreme Court

Scott C. Wilcox, "Granting Certiorari to Video Recording but Not to Televising," *Michigan Law Review First Impressions*, vol. 106, 2007, pp. 24–27. Copyright © 2007 by Scott Wilcox. Reproduced by permission of the author and the Michigan Law Review Association.

will allow the televising of its oral arguments. But until then, merely recording the arguments would give the public greater access to the Court while also addressing the justices' most pressing concerns.

Cameras are an understandable yet inept target for Supreme Court Justices apprehensive about televising the high Court's proceedings. Notwithstanding Justice [David] Souter's declaration to a congressional subcommittee in 1996 that cameras will have to roll over his dead body to enter the Court, the Justices' public statements suggest that their objections are to televising—not to cameras. In fact, welcoming cameras to video record Court proceedings for archival purposes will serve the Justices' interests well. Video recording can forestall legislation recently introduced in both houses of Congress that would require the Court to televise its proceedings. The Court's desired result—the legislation disappearing from the congressional agenda—will become more plausible once the Justices have acknowledged legislators' legitimate arguments for improving access to the Court. When initiating video recording, however, the Justices can allay the concerns they have expressed about televising by strictly limiting the distribution of the archival footage.

I propose that the Supreme Court voluntarily begin video recording its proceedings and make the footage available for viewing at the National Archives. The Court could arrange with the Archives to prohibit copying of oral argument video; visitors would be permitted to view the footage and to take notes but not to duplicate the recordings. The College Park, Maryland, branch of the Archives, accessible to anyone (but only with photo identification), serves as the federal government's multimedia depository. Traditionally, anyone can copy recordings warehoused there because government materials are generally in the public domain and fall outside the protections of copyright.

Use the National Archives as Depository

But preventing the copying of video recordings of the Court should not demand too much of the Archives. Dubbing and recording equipment is already prohibited within the Motion Picture, Sound, and Video research room's Restricted Media Viewing and Listening Area. Moreover, precedent for placing copying restrictions on government recordings, although rare, definitely exists. According to Susan Cooper, Director of Public Affairs for the U.S. National Archives and Records Administration, visitors interested in the [Richard] Nixon tapes originally were permitted only to listen to the audio recordings and to make notes; copying the tapes was at first prohibited. (Litigation over the Nixon tapes resulted in the limitations initially being placed on their distribution. Since then, most of the collection has become available for copying, but this relaxation of copying restrictions does not foreordain the eventual loosening of access to Court videos; the unique context of the Watergate-inspired criminal proceedings in *United States v. Nixon* is easily distinguished. Instead, sitting Justices would retain control over the disposition of any video recordings made as they currently do with respect to audio recordings.)

Utilizing the National Archives as a depository for Supreme Court recordings is a familiar concept for the Justices. The Court has made audio recordings of its public proceedings since 1955 and began depositing the recordings annually with the Archives in 1969. Recordings are stored in the office of the Marshal of the Supreme Court for the duration of each current term, and the Marshal transfers the term's recordings to the Archives at the beginning of the following term. After the recordings arrive at the Archives, anyone may listen to them or freely copy them. Because the Court relaxed its policy governing the copying of tapes of its proceedings in 1993, the public can now use and copy the recordings even for commercial purposes. Adding to the Justices' familiarity with the

Archives, the main Archives facility in Washington, D.C., also stores printed transcripts of Court proceedings.

The Justices' apprehension about providing fodder for television programming too often comprised of truncated soundbites will disappear.

Addressing Justices' Concerns

Because I have tailored my proposal to address the Justices' express concerns about televising, it is best evaluated in the context of the Justices' past statements about televising Court proceedings. Over the past twenty-five years, the current Justices each have reacted, at least briefly, to the concept of televising the Court's proceedings. The four Justices who outright oppose televising—[Anthony] Kennedy, [Antonin] Scalia, [Clarence] Thomas, and (as already noted) Souter—have expressed several concerns: televising may adversely affect the institution, televising would intrude on the Justices' privacy, soundbites shown on the nightly news would mislead the public about the Court's work, and televising could imprudently signal to lower courts that the Justices believe televising all federal court proceedings is advisable. Other Justices, however, have recognized the potential merits of greater public access to the Court. Justice [John Paul] Stevens, for example, expressed concern in a 1985 statement about the fact that, in many high-profile cases, members of the public were being turned away from the Supreme Court after a long wait; he alluded that television might be a solution to the problem yet acknowledged the unforeseeable impact televising might have on the Court. Justice [Ruth] Bader Ginsburg indicated in a 2000 interview that she personally had no objections to televising but that she respected the positions of her colleagues who do.

Bearing these considerations in mind, permitting cameras into the Court in order to record oral arguments for archival purposes is a modest step that will eliminate the express concerns motivating judicial opposition to televising. The Justices' apprehension about providing fodder for television programming too often comprised of truncated soundbites will disappear. (Understandably, the Justices would likely prefer to foreclose the possibility of a clip of oral arguments being featured in the *Daily Show with Jon Stewart*'s "A Moment of Zen" or in some other humorous but anti-contextual frame of reference.) While oral arguments theoretically could be viewed out of context at the Archives, this approach presents no greater danger of distortion than the "three-minute line" at the Court, which provides visitors only the briefest glimpse of the Justices at work.

Televising vs. Recording

Additional reasons given for opposing televising also fail to resonate in the different realm of archival recording. In Justice Thomas's March 2007 testimony before a congressional subcommittee, he vocalized some Justices' privacy concerns. Their apprehensions, it seems, stem from a belief that regular television coverage of Court proceedings will erode the relative anonymity that a few Justices have managed to preserve. Archival recording, however, avoids widespread media exposure and will impact the Justices' privacy and security minimally, if at all. Also, because the footage will no longer be released for media distribution, the worry that the Supreme Court might indicate to lower courts that televising is advisable in all cases will also evaporate.

Archival recording should mollify even Justices who have expressed the concern that televising will negatively affect the character of oral arguments. The limited distribution of archival footage should allay most fears that video recording will exacerbate this problem. Even if a few arguing counsels are tempted to overly dramatize their arguments for the cameras, most Supreme Court litigators will exercise self-restraint out of respect for the Court, especially once they recognize the film will not be airing on the 11 p.m. news.

Greater Access than Television

While my proposal will likely address the Justices' concerns, substituting archival recording for televising may fail to satisfy many advocates of greater media access to the Court. Admittedly, financial and time constraints will prevent some prospective viewers of the archived oral arguments from traveling to the depository at the Archives. This reality is a consequence of our federal system, one in which many government institutions are located in the Washington, D.C., metropolitan area. The John F. Kennedy Center for the Performing Arts and the Smithsonian Institution are merely two examples. But the availability of Court video on demand at the Archives may afford to many other viewers even greater access than if the footage instead were televised on a fixed schedule. Television coverage is most likely to air within the days or weeks after Court proceedings are recorded, whereas archival footage will be accessible for the foreseeable future. Moreover, acknowledging the inadequacy of archival recording for some purposes does not undercut the great benefits that access to the recordings will bring to historians, legal practitioners, law students, and even the media. Video recordings of oral argument will prove invaluable resources as law students and practitioners study Supreme Court advocacy, as legal scholars study the Court's jurisprudence, and as historians study the Justices and the operation of the Court. This value should not be surprising because oral arguments offer a rare glimpse into the inner workings of a largely private Court and into the inner minds of the nine individuals who guide our nation's jurisprudence. To be sure, transcripts and audio recordings are valuable. But oral arguments take place in three dimensions, and the next best thing to experiencing them live is watching a video. Video can capture the nuances of communication—among the Justices as well as between the Justices and counsel—that tend to be understated in transcripts and even in audio recordings. The Court should not overlook these benefits to society when they easily may be attained without sacrificing the Justices' control over the Court's proceedings.

In light of the value of archival recording, expanding the Archives' Supreme Court collection surely will increase the attractiveness of the depository to scholars, students of the Court, budding advocates, and interested members of the public. The Archives already are popular destinations, drawing over a million visitors each year. Of course, the majority of visitors tour the main Archives in Washington, D.C., which house the original Declaration of Independence, Constitution, and Bill of Rights. Nevertheless the College Park branch housing the multimedia depository, which is conveniently located only ten miles outside of Washington, D.C., also draws significant numbers of visitors.

Video recording should be both judicially acceptable and politically achievable.

A Reasonable Compromise

Notwithstanding the skepticism that this proposal may face from advocates for televising the Court, it is the most viable means of achieving greater access to the Court at present. The current Court seems unwilling to consider televising its proceedings voluntarily, and the political and constitutional viability of the legislation pending in both houses of Congress is uncertain. But video recording should be both judicially acceptable and politically achievable.

The Court may fear that allowing archival cameras would only strengthen the position of those advocating the televising of oral arguments, but this concern is misplaced. Justices have shared their concerns about televising with Congress in no uncertain terms. Congress will likely defer to the Justices once the Court has acknowledged legitimate arguments for improving access to its proceedings, even if the Justices take only this incremental step. Legislators will not lightly provoke a constitutional showdown with the Supreme Court, and most will be unwilling to do so when the Court has supplemented its reasoned defense of continued non-televising with archival recording. Even if a minority of legislators feels that requiring the Court to distribute its video footage would be a more natural exercise of congressional power than would be forcing the Court to permit the installation of cameras, such reasoning is unlikely to carry the day—especially in light of several Justices having made an impassioned appeal to Congress to respect the Court's perspective and purview.

Eventually, the Supreme Court may be ready to air the highest (and most consequential) reality television show in the land. Until such time, however, video recording will allow the Court to document for posterity the most public aspect of its important work without compromising the character and dignity of the Court's proceedings. This simple step will also stave off an undesirable conflict between the Supreme Court and the other branches. Stay tuned for further developments.

7

Cameras in Courtrooms Would Trivialize Court Proceedings

Woody West

Woody West is a former associate editor of the Washington Times.

In 2003, judges denied access to TV cameras in three high-profile cases—the trials of the two Washington, D.C.–area sniper suspects and a capital case in Texas. These judges deserve praise for their decisions, especially in today's camera-happy culture. Those who advocate for cameras in courtrooms say that they lead to a better-educated public. While this is a virtuous aim, in reality, TV cameras in the courtroom lead to a cultural trivialization of such proceedings, reducing our judicial process to the level of petty reality shows like Survivor.

A round of applause, please, for the judges who have rejected TV cameras in three high-visibility criminal cases. Two of these cases are in Virginia—the separate pending trials of [Lee Boyd Malvo and John Allen Muhammad] the pair charged with homicide during the vicious sniper shootings that terrorized the Washington [D.C.] area and several states and left at least 10 persons killed and three wounded [in October 2002]. The third instance is in Texas, where public television thought it would be dandy to videotape jury deliberations in a capital case.

Woody West, "Will TV Cameras Turn Trials into *Survivor?*" *Insight on the News*, vol. 19, April 1–14, 2003, p. 56. Copyright © 2003 News World Communications, Inc. All rights reserved. Reproduced with permission of *Insight*.

The camera has insinuated itself into nearly every cranny of the culture, the bedroom not excluded. Indeed, we now live—heaven help us—in a social environment dominated by the electronic media. A cable channel [Court TV, now called truTV] devoted to court cases illustrates how thoroughly the justice system has been penetrated.

The solemn rationale is that TV cameras "demystify" and result in a better-informed citizenry. It is, instead, a perverse form of entertainment (the O.J. [Simpson murder] trial [in 1995], of course, is a conspicuous example). All 50 states now permit courtroom cameras under varying conditions, though only 37 allow them in criminal cases. Never mind the expressed justifications, televised trials are another slicing away of respect for fragile institutions. These subtractions deform the open society in which restraint is part of liberty.

The arguments on behalf of courtroom cameras are not frivolous. Routine use of television in such a solemn context, however, emphasizes the radical egalitarianism that defers to no one or no thing. A camera significantly if subtly transforms its field of vision and those in it, no matter how carefully controlled; a camera cannot help but trivialize that on which it focuses by introducing a starkly artificial element. There remain pockets of resistance to cameras in the courtroom—the Supreme Court notably. May it ever stand fast against allowing the ubiquitous lens in the august chamber.

Preserving the Court's Dignity

Regretfully, to argue against the practice is a losing battle for the most part for those who contend that the justice system must retain a degree of aloofness to preserve what dignity yet endures—and dignity increasingly is a casualty of the politicization of the judiciary.

Thus, it is heartening that cameras have been prohibited in the pending trials (summary execution now being generally frowned upon) of the pair charged in [2002's] vicious sniper killings. Lee Boyd Malvo, 18, is to be tried in November [2003] in Fairfax County, Va. A phalanx of network and cable-TV reporters . . . recently asked Judge Jane Marum Roush to permit them to broadcast the trial, and newspapers asked that still photography be permitted.

"The public's right to know" [is] a "right" that is not enunciated in the Constitution.

"I am concerned with the possible prejudice to Mr. Malvo of photography—whether still or television," the judge said recently in rejecting the requests. Prosecutors opposing the motion raised a dramatically critical objection: the possible effect on jurors—and that shouldn't need elaboration. The judge did give permission for a closed-circuit feed into a county building for relatives of victims, reporters, investigators and members of the public who can elbow their way in.

Malvo's suspected accomplice, John Allen Muhammad, is to go on trial in adjacent Prince William County for one of the sniper slayings there and, likewise, the court also tossed out requests for cameras.

It was not unexpected that newspapers and broadcasters would emote loudly and at length to open these courtrooms under the noble rubric of "the public's right to know"—a "right" that is not enunciated in the Constitution. It is as expected, too, that the media will continue to pry at courtroom doors, notwithstanding the failure in these instances.

Cameras Corrupt and Trivialize

The Texas foray by the press, however, is so bizarre that only a tax-subsidized, quasi-governmental body, the Public Broadcasting [Service, or PBS], would have essayed it. *Frontline*, a PBS series, pleaded to be allowed to videotape a jury in a murder trial when it convened to reach a verdict. A Texas district-court judge [in 2002] agreed that a *Frontline* documentary crew could poke its cameras into the jury room in the case of a 17-year-old being tried for killing a man in a carjacking.

A camera could corrupt jury deliberations, inhibiting some jurors.

A lower-court judge in Houston granted the PBS request. Prosecutors appealed to the state's highest criminal court [in March 2003], arguing against the supposed justification for admitting television—that a camera could shed valuable light on the death-penalty process. Among other contentions, prosecutors cited the shatteringly obvious: A camera could corrupt jury deliberations, inhibiting some jurors, bringing out the exhibitionist in others before the recording lens. (Proponents of courtroom TV adamantly contend that studies show cameras do not have this effect—which studies should be regarded with wry skepticism.)

In its 6-3 decision, the Texas Court of Criminal Appeals ruled that videotaping the deliberations, which would have been a first in a U.S. capital case, would violate the "ancient and centuries-old rule that jury deliberations should be private and confidential." That this goofy gambit was spawned in the provinces of public broadcasting is alone sufficient to end all taxpayer money for PBS, a move long overdue.

The most dispiriting part of the case was an observation by one of the judges on the Texas high criminal court that permitting a camera inside a jury room would turn deliberations into "reality TV, like *Survivor*"—the bottom of television's most odious barrel.

8

Cameras in Courtrooms Would Lead to a More Educated Public

Sandy Grady

Sandy Grady is a former columnist for the Philadelphia Daily News. *She is currently a member of the* USA Today *board of contributors.*

The Supreme Court has never made its arguments public, despite the fact that forty-seven states allow cameras into their trials. The Supreme Court's ban on cameras is downright undemocratic. After all, the Founding Fathers explicitly stated that courtrooms should be large enough to accommodate the public. In addition, congressional sessions have been made available to the public via C-SPAN, a development that has had a positive effect on the decorum of those proceedings. Contrary to critics' fears that cameras will trivialize the judicial process, there is clearly an educational benefit to the broadcasting of such proceedings. Perhaps the Supreme Court justices resist the appearance of cameras in their court out of a desire for privacy. Given the significance of the Court's decisions, however, it is only right that the American public be allowed to watch the Supreme Court at work.

You might say Judge John Roberts is history's first made-for-TV nominee for the Supreme Court. With his smooth, bland face and careful haircut, he seems to burst fresh from a barbershop or makeup room. He speaks in concise sentences. He rarely loses his sincere, benign smile. If this gig doesn't work out, he could get work as a TV anchorman.

Roberts seems created for his star role this week [September 2005] as network TV cameras focus on his grilling by the Senate Judiciary Committee. He is a conservative with the demeanor of a friendly scoutmaster. Barring edgy surprises, he will likely cool the red-state-blue-state [Republican/ Democratic] furor and be drafted to be the youngest chief justice since 1806.

And then—presto, shazam!—Roberts will disappear. This made-for-TV paragon with the camera-ready stylishness of a [news anchor such as] Dan Rather, Peter Jennings or Tom Brokaw will vanish from television. Roberts will sink into the cloistered maw of a Supreme Court whose black-robed deities treat TV cameras as welcome as an anthrax attack. Since the justices first met in 1790, no camera has shown their arguments to the public.

Never mind that 47 states allow cameras into trials. Never mind that we can play voyeur at the televised reality soap operas of Martha Stewart [businesswoman and TV homemaking advocate convicted of conspiracy and obstructing justice in 2004], Michael Jackson [entertainer tried and acquitted of child molestation charges in 2005], Kobe Bryant [basketball star whose rape case was dismissed in 2004], Scott Peterson [convicted of killing his pregnant wife and unborn son in 2004] and the latest runaway bride.

Undeniably, there's educational benefit to those TV trials along with the celebrity pizzazz. But if you want to watch the nation's highest court interrogate lawyers and argue such crucial issues as abortion, immigration, gun control or post-9/11 prisoners, forget it. That is, unless you have time to line up outside the Supreme Court for a three-minute glimpse inside.

For the Supremes stuck in their 19th-century fustiness to ban TV cameras at their ornate doors is, I think, an undemocratic shame.

TV Covers Congress

The U.S. House of Representatives since 1977, the Senate since 1986, White House news conferences and almost all Washington events are open to cameras (usually those of C-SPAN). Time for the Supremes to also drop their tech-phobia and join the 21st century. Maybe Roberts, so slickly adept at the electronic stage, can change the justices' shy ways if he joins them. Sen. Arlen Specter, R-Pa., who has long pushed for TV in the court, said of Roberts, "He may have a little different view about television. He's a new generation."

Even so, Roberts would have a tough sale. Time after time, the Supremes have reacted to TV coverage as if it would transform them into a tawdry *Jerry Springer Show*. Justice David Souter told a House subcommittee that TV cameras would be allowed "over my dead body." The late chief justice William Rehnquist had groused that the cameras would lessen the Court's "mystique and moral authority." We can guess at the opposition of Judge Antonin Scalia, who bars cameras or taping of his public appearances—a marshal grabbed a reporter's recorder at a Scalia oration on free speech.

The Founding Fathers . . . wanted courtrooms large enough for "as many of the people as choose to attend."

But wait a minute. The Founding Fathers, according to the resolves of the First Continental Congress, wanted courtrooms large enough for "as many of the people as choose to attend." If you're going to invite 300 million people, that means TV. The great Oliver Wendell Holmes, long before invention of the remote control, said the judiciary should be open so that each citizen is "able to satisfy himself within his own eyes" how judges perform.

Modern camera-phobic justices, however, consider TV a nosy, vulgar threat to their dignity. They fret that cameras would change the behavior of lawyers who appear at their lectern or the justices themselves, causing grandstanding for ideological applause. They worry about bright lights. And about networks using TV snippets to slant the news.

Misplaced Concerns

Those seem false fears. I covered the House and Senate when C-SPAN turned on its cameras. If anything, speech and decorum improved. (No more slurred bloviating after three-martini lunches.) The televised Senate impeachment trial of Bill Clinton, over which Rehnquist presided, was unaffected by cameras. C-SPAN, master of discreet camera work, has offered to televise the Supremes' arguments start to finish without comment. Surveys of states report no ill effect from televised courts (let's forget the O.J. Simpson [1995 murder trial] carnival).

When [the Supreme Court] makes momentous decisions . . . we all should have front-row seats via television.

No, I suspect the real hang-up for the Supremes against cameras is their desperate clinging to privacy. They relish their cocoon of facelessness—to go to a mall unobserved.

I saw this personally one afternoon on a golf course when I was joined by a lean, strong-handed 70-year-old whom I recognized instantly as Justice Byron (Whizzer) White. I guessed he wanted to be incognito. Only after a quiet nine holes did I say, "Didn't you play football at Colorado?"

White looked horrified. "How did you recognize me?" he snapped. Then he mumbled, "Well, it was Monday and the court wasn't busy so . . . look, I've got to go!" He fled for his car.

That's the real angst of the Supremes toward cameras in their court—up their precious anonymity. But the high court isn't some imperious, autocratic mystery cult divorced from American life. When it makes momentous decisions—especially the 5-4 vote that stopped the Florida recount and gave George W. Bush the presidency—we all should have front-row seats via television. . . .

As its new chief, maybe John G. Roberts Jr., with his salesman's flair and anchorman's ease on the tube, can persuade the justices to lose their paranoia toward TV cameras.

Mr. Chief Justice Roberts, . . . open up those doors and let the rest of America inside.

9

Reluctance to Use Cameras in Courtrooms Is a Result of the Simpson Trial

Ellia Thompson

Ellia Thompson is an associate attorney at Jeffer Mangels Butler and Marmaro LLP in Los Angeles. In 2004, as a law student, she was a Pulliam/Kilgore Freedom of Information intern at the Society of Professional Journalists.

Judges in several recent high-profile trials, including those of accused terrorist Zacarias Moussaoui and entertainer Michael Jackson, have banned cameras from their courtrooms. These prohibitions highlight a trend that dates back to 1965 but appeared to come to an end in 1981 when the Supreme Court ruled that a ban on broadcast coverage of judicial proceedings would be unconstitutional. But the 1995 murder trial of former football star O.J. Simpson, televised in its entirety, amounted to a media circus, according to many. Judge Lance Ito's apparent inability to control his own courtroom led many judges and legislators to impose bans on courtroom coverage, many of which remain in effect today. Judges in recent trials have cited concerns about the defendant's right to a fair trial and, in the case of Moussaoui, the security of trial participants. Yet advocates of cameras in courtrooms have remained strong, perhaps even emboldened by these setbacks. Finally, there are signs that the freezing effect of the Simpson trial on media coverage of courtrooms is beginning to subside.

Ellia Thompson, "Courtroom Cameras: Issue Moves In and Out of Focus," *The Quill*, vol. 92, September 2004, pp. 7–10. Copyright © 2004 Society of Professional Journalists. Reproduced by permission.

The alleged "20th hijacker" in the Sept. 11, 2001, terrorist attacks [Zacarias Moussaoui] is indicted.

The trials of two of the United States' most notorious serial killers [Lee Boyd Malvo and John Allen Muhammad], who terrorized a region for weeks by shooting victims randomly with high-powered rifles, takes place in separate courtrooms.

One of the world's most famous pop stars [Michael Jackson] is arraigned by a grand jury on charges of molesting young boys.

What do these cases have in common?

The daily judicial proceedings of each criminal trial were or will be shielded from most Americans.

Television cameras continue to be banned in most American courtrooms—state and federal—despite the fact that each state has a law permitting cameras in the courtroom, usually at the judge's discretion. Many believe the impact of television coverage of the O.J. Simpson murder trial immeasurably set back a move toward allowing cameras in court proceedings. Nevertheless, progress has been made in recent years, and there is much the media can do to ensure that progress continues. . . .

But understanding how we arrived at camera usage in 2004 requires a look at the past.

The movement to obtain broadcast coverage of trials suffered its first substantial blow in 1965, when the U.S. Supreme Court in *Billie Sol Estes v. Texas* found that a criminal defendant was denied due process of law as a result of the television coverage of his trial.

Although the Supreme Court did not rule that television coverage was inherently unconstitutional, it objected to the "circus atmosphere" created by the numerous cameras, lights and other broadcast equipment at the trial.

However, as cameras became less obtrusive more states began to permit coverage. In the early 1980s, two monumental cases in favor of cameras in the courtroom appeared to propel the movement forward.

Gains in Movement for Cameras in Court

In 1980, the Supreme Court in *Richmond Newspaper Inc. v. Virginia*, rejected a trial judge's decision to close a criminal trial to the public and media, held that a criminal courtroom is a public place in which the presence of the public and media historically has been thought to enhance the integrity and quality of the proceedings.

The next year in *Chandler v. Florida*, the Supreme Court finally considered whether television coverage of criminal trials violates defendants' rights per se, even when it does not create a circus-like atmosphere, and found that it does not.

The Supreme Court ruled: "The risk of juror prejudice in some cases does not . . . warrant an absolute constitutional bar on all broadcast coverage." The Supreme Court also affirmed the right of each state to permit electronic and still photographic coverage of criminal trials without the consent of the accused.

The fallout from the [O.J.] Simpson trial was immediate and widespread.

Subsequently, many states dropped bans on electronic media, while others began experimenting with the use of cameras in the courtroom.

"When we started Court TV back in 1991, about half the states allowed cameras in the courtroom, and by 1995 it went to about two-thirds," said Fred Graham, chief anchor and managing editor of Court TV.

"The phenomenon of having cameras in the courtroom and gavel-to-gavel coverage was very successful. The public was very receptive, and the judicial officials felt it was positive."

Simpson Trial a Major Setback

But a decade ago [1994], NFL [National Football League] running back O.J. Simpson was charged with murder in the slayings of his wife and her male friend, and the nation was permitted to view the trial from start to finish.

Presiding Judge Lance Ito was seen by some as unable to control the behavior of the prosecuting and defense attorneys. Lawyers on both sides were accused of grandstanding and playing to the cameras, both in the courtroom and outside on the steps during "impromptu" press conferences. The fallout from the Simpson trial was immediate and widespread. Among the casualties was the impetus to allow cameras into the nation's courtrooms.

- In California, then-Gov. Pete Wilson launched an unsuccessful campaign to ban television coverage of trials in the state, citing a need "to preserve the integrity of the judicial process."

- In Connecticut, a bill that would have expanded media access to allow coverage of executions did not pass.

- Individual judges also took action to bar the media from courtrooms. A Sonoma County, Calif., superior court judge, citing the "media saturation" of the O.J. Simpson trial, granted the requests of both sides and refused to permit live or still cameras during the trial of Richard Allen Davis. Davis was accused of the kidnapping and murder of [twelve-year-old] Polly Klaas.

- Just three days after the Simpson verdict, Lyle Menendez's attorney persuaded Los Angeles County Superior Court Judge Stanley M. Weisberg to change his mind and ban live coverage [of the trial of Menendez, who, along with his brother, was accused of killing his parents].

Momentum to obtain access for cameras in the federal courts also stalled.

In May 1990, U.S. Rep. Robert Kastenmeier, D-Wis., then chairman of the House Judiciary Committee's subcommittee on the courts, had written to the Judicial Conference that "it is timely for the federal courts, at both the trial and appellate levels, to permit electronic and photographic news coverage in the courtroom."

The next year a pilot program allowing cameras in the courts was conducted in civil and appellate courts. The federal pilot program lasted three years, and camera access was granted to about 200 proceedings. An extensive study conducted by the judiciary's own research arm, the Federal Judicial Center, found that the reaction to the pilot programs was favorable.

Aftermath of the Simpson Trial

However, rather than continuing the experiment, the Judicial Conference approved a nationwide ban on federal trial court camera coverage.

The Judicial Conference permitted cameras in circuit courts that chose to permit them, but so far, the 2nd and 9th Circuits are the only ones to do so.

Tony Mauro, Supreme Court correspondent for *Legal Times* and American Lawyer Media, covered the federal courts during this time and believed that things might have proceeded differently if not for the Simpson trial.

"The experiment in the early 1990s to allow cameras in a few appellate courts was pretty positive," he said. "The Judicial Conference was debating whether to continue the experiment at the same time the O.J. trial was getting under way. (But) the members of the committee were so shell-shocked by the antics going on in that trial that they decided not to go forward."

The worst fears of those who oppose cameras in courtrooms materialized during coverage of the Simpson trial.

Though the worst fears of those who oppose cameras in courtrooms materialized during coverage of the Simpson trial the experience at the same time strengthened the convictions of camera advocates.

"Cameras only showed the truth of what was really going on in the courtroom," said Judge Ted Poe, a widely respected Texas criminal judge who has served on the bench for 22 years and who presided over more than 1,000 cases.

"Judge Ito lost control of the trial. All the cameras did was show that. Unfortunately, (today) people gauge the criminal justice system on that one trial."

In 2002, Poe made history when he fought to allow producers of the PBS documentary series "Frontline" to cover jury deliberations in the capital murder trial of a 17-year-old.

Ultimately, the Texas Court of Criminal Appeals stymied Poe's efforts, holding that the presence of a camera in the jury room "violates the cardinal principle that the deliberations of the jury shall remain private and secret in every case."

Advocates Remain Strong

But Poe continues to advocate the benefits of cameras to a wide array of court proceedings.

"(I) continue to believe that serving on a jury frightens most people," he states on his Web site. "But if more people understood the process, possibly they would not try to avoid jury duty and be more willing to take the responsibility seriously."

Educating the public and fostering government accountability are the most common defenses cited by camera advocates.

As U.S. District Court Judge Nancy Gertner of Massachusetts testified at a Senate hearing in September 2000: "At a time when polls suggest that the public is woefully misinformed about the justice system, more information, and relatively unmediated information, is better than less information."

Supporters also say that an open system raises public confidence in the judicial system and can help maintain peace in an embittered community. After Amadou Diallo, an unarmed West African man living in the Bronx, N.Y., was gunned down by four police officers, New York Supreme Court Judge Joseph Teresi permitted Court TV to televise the proceedings of the ensuing trial of the four New York Police Department officers in order to enable the entire community to view the proceedings.

Far more often than they grant them, judges deny requests to permit cameras in the courtroom.

Many legal experts attributed the lack of anticipated rioting after the acquittals were announced to Teresi's decision to allow television coverage.

"The Judge thought it was important for folks in the Bronx to see what was going on with the case since it had been moved to Albany," said Kathleen Kirby, counsel to the Radio and Television News Directors Association [RTNDA]. "Court TV broadcast the entire trial, and it was clear by the time the jury reached a verdict that the prosecutors had never made their case, which in turn, helped squelch any incentive to riot."

However, judges such as Teresi and Poe are in the minority.

Effects on Recent Trials

Far more often than they grant them, judges deny requests to permit cameras in the courtroom.

In the trial of Scott Peterson for the murder of his wife and unborn child, Judge Alfred Delucchi refused requests to allow cameras in the courtroom during the preliminary hearing or trial.

Delucchi cited the need to protect Peterson's right to a fair trial and the privacy rights of witnesses and victims in the case.

Concern over the defendant's right to a fair trial also led Virginia Circuit Judge Jane Marum Roush to prohibit cameras in her courtroom for the trial of Lee [Boyd] Malvo, one of the sniper suspects.

And in recent years, security issues have increasingly motivated judges to close proceedings to the broadcast media.

Such concerns were prominent in the debate over media coverage of the trial of Zacarias Moussaoui, the suspected "20th hijacker" in the September 11, 2001, terrorist attacks. Although the proceedings are in federal court—which currently bans cameras filming or televising any court proceeding—media organizations asked U.S. District Judge Leonie Brinkema to overturn the ban, stressing the extraordinary national and international public interest in the case.

Brinkema denied the media's motions, citing "significant concerns about the security of trial participants and the integrity of the fact finding."

Many opponents of cameras in courtrooms also argue cameras are disruptive to the judicial process, a concern that has changed but not necessarily lessened with advances in technology.

Though cameras have become less intrusive, the Internet has broadened the audience for trial coverage and heightened concerns that parties, lawyers or witnesses will play to the cameras.

As Brinkema noted: "(Worldwide) broadcasting of these proceedings, either by television, radio or the Internet, would be an open invitation to any trial participant to engage in showmanship or make a public spectacle for the world to see and hear."

New Technology, New Opportunities

However, for others, technology offers the opportunity to truly provide public access to court proceedings.

Until July 2004, Wise County, Va., Circuit Court maintained a webcast of all of its court proceedings. The court has since switched to cable, which brings video of its court proceedings to 100,000 to 150,000 viewers.

"We believe in open government as a principle that applies to all three branches of government," said Clerk of Court Jack Kennedy. "The judicial branch is far too often clouded in a fog of obscurity. Our principles of open government demand that we provide access to our constituents."

The judicial system, from the top down, appears to be starting to embrace this concept.

In *Bush v. Gore* in December 2000, the Supreme Court for the first time allowed audio recordings of the oral arguments to be broadcast to the public on the same day.

Advocates of camera access hope that the Supreme Court's recent move is a beginning, not an end.

Since then, the Supreme Court has allowed the speedy release of audiotapes in several high-profile cases, including:

- The landmark affirmative action cases in 2003

- Cases [in 2004] addressing the rights of prisoners in the U.S. Navy prison camp in [Guantánamo Bay] Cuba

- The public's right of access to information about closed-door meetings of Vice President [Dick] Cheney's energy coalition. Advocates of camera access hope that the Supreme Court's recent move is a beginning, not an end.

"Although having audio feeds of oral arguments in front of the Supreme Court was a good thing," said Mauro, "the downside is that the Supreme Court may have done all it wants to do in terms of recognizing the 21st century and may not take another step toward technology until we enter the 22nd century."

Meanwhile, the issue of cameras in state courts has gained momentum in legislatures and courtrooms throughout the country in recent years.

In July 2001, South Dakota became the 50th state to allow cameras in at least some of its courtrooms. The state Supreme Court announced that it would allow video and audio coverage of oral arguments during its sessions.

The success in South Dakota was largely a result of journalists' efforts to educate judges.

"In South Dakota, the state supreme court justices met with one of our members and carefully planned a way they could experiment with cameras and determined that they are not disruptive in courtrooms," said RTNDA President Barbara Cochran. "The same thing is happening in Indiana. When journalists can show a judge in one state how well cameras in the courtroom work in another state, they can be persuasive."

Court TV's Graham concurred that journalists can be effective in reaching out to hesitant judges.

"Something that we did was videotape our camera crews setting up in a courtroom and narrated the tape explaining what the process was and how nondisruptive the equipment is," he said.

"We send these tapes to judges who are considering whether to allow cameras in their courtroom."

"Since *Billie Sol Estes v. Texas*, no verdict has been overturned because of cameras in the courtroom. It's that kind of argument we can make."

Journalists Can Educate Judges

Continuing education programs also provide an opportunity for reporters to meet with judges and discuss the benefits and solve the problems related to camera coverage of trials.

The National Judicial College in Reno, Nev., has a program with its National Center for Courts and the Media that offers training to state trial justices as well as courtroom staff such as public affairs officers. In the program, judges learn about First Amendment issues from reporters and gain insight in striking a proper balance between protection of the public's First Amendment rights and individuals' Sixth Amendment right to a fair trial.

The program for courtroom personnel offers instruction on how to deal with the media in high-profile cases.

This summer [2004], the National Judicial College provided its first training for journalists assigned to cover trials.

In August, it trained 50 to 55 journalists to cover the courts, said Gary Hengstler, the Director of the National Center for Courts and the Media. "The biggest criticism that we hear from judges about journalists is that they don't understand the general procedures of a courtroom, let alone the subtle, but important nuances of a trial," Hengstler said.

10

Cameras Should Be Allowed at High-Profile Trials

Howard Rosenberg

Howard Rosenberg is a retired TV critic for the Los Angeles Times, *where he won a Pulitzer Prize for Criticism. He is currently a columnist at* Broadcasting & Cable *magazine, where he has covered numerous television-related events, including Michael Jackson's 2005 child molestation trial.*

Presiding superior court judge Rodney S. Melville has banned TV cameras from the courtroom where entertainer Michael Jackson undergoes a trial for child molestation in Santa Maria, California. The judge has said he is trying to prevent the trial from becoming a media circus. But because there is such wide public interest in the trial, and the public will undoubtedly be enlightened by seeing it, cameras should be allowed. In fact, cameras inside courtrooms generally do not interfere with trials. In the infamous O.J. Simpson trial, the media circus took place outside the courtroom rather than inside. Furthermore, limiting reporters' access to courtrooms means less comprehensive and often less accurate coverage of such trials.

California is among 47 states that allow trials to be televised. Yet no TV camera is allowed in the courtroom as Michael Jackson faces child molestation charges [in 2005] in coastal Santa Maria.

Howard Rosenberg, "Let TV Go to the Circus," *Broadcasting & Cable*, vol. 135, March 7, 2005, p. 50. Copyright © 2005 Reed Business Information, a division of Reed Elsevier. Republished with permission of Broadcasting & Cable, conveyed through Copyright Clearance Center, Inc.

The reason? Presiding Superior Court Judge Rodney S. Melville doesn't want Jackson's trial—hold your laughter—to become the circus of the century.

No courtroom camera, no Big Top? Puh-leeeeeze!

As the trial gets under way, it is time to debate again the question of allowing cameras in the courtrooms, a crossroads of the 1st and 6th Amendments, where some believe freedom of expression and the public's right to know collide with a citizen's right to a fair and speedy trial.

This is a valid concern. Yet the Jackson trial should be televised because, simply put, there is wide public interest and no compelling argument against it. There is, however, a big argument in favor of it: public enlightenment.

A camera isn't needed in Jackson's courtroom, one might argue, given that E! Entertainment and Rupert Murdoch's British satellite service BSkyB will provide their own trial accounts by having actors read testimony from the previous day's transcript, just as E! did during O.J. Simpson's civil trial. But although the words will be accurate, missing will be the tone of the testimony and overall courtroom ambience. It is still phony.

It was outside *the O.J. courtroom that media kazoos tooted off-key and TV-ready lawyers scored the trial like a sporting event.*

As Court TV affirms, telecasts of actual criminal trials have the potential to smarten viewers about a process few of them will ever encounter in person. So the Jackson trial won't be typical? So it will be salacious? So what! It will be what it is.

O.J. Trial Aftermath

Rarely do TV cameras inside courtrooms harm high-profile trials. This is true despite the camera's bad rap at O.J.

Simpson's criminal trial. Judge Lance Ito lost control of that courtroom, but the cameras were blamed for the chaos. The result was a lingering backlash, causing judges to be more camera-wary in recent years.

These judges need to be reminded that it was *outside* the O.J. courtroom that media kazoos tooted off-key and TV-ready lawyers scored the trial like a sporting event. And the sawdust is hitting the fan once again just outside the Santa Barbara County Courthouse. This is Ringlingville, where the jugglers, trapeze artists and floppy-shoed, fright-wigged, bulb-nosed clowns of media are gathered.

Only a handful of press members are actually inside the 160-seat courtroom. Yet more than 1,000 have signed on for Michael Madness in a coastal town that surely has more homely strip malls per square foot than any other community in California. To say nothing, these days, of satellite dishes, portable toilets for media and newly erected platforms for anchors.

Beside the courthouse is a narrow corridor marked off for 17 satellite trucks. And behind a six-foot security fence are spaces allotted to more than 50 TV crews from as far away as France and Japan, another chain-link barrier separating them from expected throngs of screaming Jackson groupies.

How curious that directly behind the courts complex sits a quaint anomaly known as the Santa Maria Lawn Bowling Club. On a recent sunny morning, elderly bowlers strode across the green in slow motion compared with the frenzied buzz of media abutting them, with sound-bite-desperate reporters pouncing on locals when not quizzing each other.

"I was interviewed by this feller from Norway," said a creaky oldster named Skip. "Or was it Australia?" Not that it matters. A circus is a circus in any language.

There is a long history of media misbehavior at sensational trials, at least as far back as the manic newsreels and brutalizing print headlines surrounding Bruno Hauptmann's 1935 conviction for the murder of Charles Lindbergh's infant son.

No credible evidence supports the claim that those inside the courtroom either turn off or on in response to the camera.

Ban on Cameras

Consequently, cameras remain banned from federal criminal trials, and only rarely are federal civil actions televised. The cameras-in-courtrooms paranoia is fed by the U.S. Supreme Court, which stubbornly refuses to allow its hearings to be televised, denying the public an opportunity to witness the nation's highest legal body at work. What are these robed sages hiding?

Opponents of cameras in courtrooms insist they inhibit participants or transform others—witnesses, lawyers, judges and even juries—into actors performing for the lens.

No credible evidence supports the claim that those inside the courtroom either turn off or on in response to the camera. And since when, in fact, do trial attorneys require a camera to encourage them to vamp? Don't they always do that to impress juries?

Foes of cameras in courtrooms also note that even responsible newscasts air the most titillating sound bites from televised trials, distorting coverage.

But that charge is as applicable to print reporters who haven't space to regurgitate entire trial transcripts and instead risk taking testimony out of context when deciding what to include and omit.

No one advocates barring print reporters from courtrooms. Why discriminate against TV?

11

Cameras Should Not Be Allowed at High-Profile Trials

Matthew Gilbert

Matthew Gilbert is the television critic for the Boston Globe.

Cameras should not be allowed in courtrooms during high-profile celebrity trials. American culture has become far too voyeuristic, with many formerly private activities considered fair game for television viewing. Representatives of the broadcasting industry say that cameras in the courtroom lead to more accurate coverage because they allow viewers to see the trial through their own eyes rather than a reporter's. But cameras do not guarantee accuracy or a comprehensive picture of the trial, and most viewers need experts to help explain what is going on in the courtroom. Champions of cameras in courtrooms also claim that cameras guarantee that a trial is being conducted fairly. Yet even without cameras, there are always people in a courtroom to monitor the proceedings. Cameras are not needed to guarantee justice or accuracy in reporting; they merely promote those aspects of our culture that need to be harnessed, not encouraged.

There are Americans, it turns out, who wish we'd seen courtroom zoom-ins of Martha Stewart's composed angst [in her conspiracy trial], who have longed to watch defendant Scott Peterson [convicted of killing his pregnant wife and unborn son] squirm, who actually want more wall-to-wall coverage of the off-the-wall Michael Jackson [acquitted of child molestation charges]. There are Americans who fear the quieting of [basketball star] Kobe Bryant's upcoming sexual assault case, who grieve the media blackout on testimony in the upcoming [actor] Robert Blake murder trial.

I'm not one of them. In recent months, in the dawning of a year [2004] that will be notable for its celebrity trials, a number of state judges have put restrictions on the media coverage of their high-profile cases. And I thank those judges, not just as a TV critic who'd rather not have to study the iconography of Jackson's eye makeup, but as a person who finds the bottomless tabloid joy in celebrity woes woeful.

Our democratic right to know about these trials, through newspaper and TV coverage, does not mean we need to sleep, eat, and breathe images from them for months at a time, following them as we have followed the soapy traumas of the "Real World" roommates, dissecting the evidence as if we were playing a board game. In the age of reality TV, as cameras transform even the most humiliating moments into sensationalized entertainment, it's reassuring to hear a few lone voices saying "no cameras."

Each judge who is forbidding live courtroom footage—at pretrial hearings (Bryant), during testimony (Blake), in any part of the trial (Peterson), or at the arraignment (Jackson)— has his or her own reasons for making that decision. Some of these robed ones want to avoid a media circus, and others have what Court TV anchor and managing editor Fred Graham calls "Ito-phobia—a fear of looking as bad as Judge [Lance] Ito did in the O.J. Simpson case." The former are protecting their trial from camera-loving lawyers and intimidated witnesses, the latter are protecting themselves from public embarrassment.

Voyeuristic Culture

Either way, I also see the judges protecting us from our own camera-centrism, our obsession with video access to everything from the awkward meetings on "Blind Date" and the violent arrests on "Cops" to the explicit description of Jackson's alleged molestation.

Cameras aren't allowed in federal courtrooms, which is why we were spared images of Stewart's sobbing assistant, for instance, as she testified against her boss. And yet the media covered the Stewart trial extensively, even interviewing jury members after they'd delivered their verdict. I do not feel at all deprived of information about the case, even if there will never be a "Saturday Night Live" spoof of the tearful assistant, even if all we got for visuals were courtroom sketches and courthouse exits and entrances. It was enough—more than enough, really—to see daily accounts in newspapers, on the 6 o'clock news, on "Entertainment Weekly," and on "Celebrity Justice."

Barbara Cochran completely disagrees.

"Rather than somebody telling you what happened," says Cochran, president of the Radio-Television News Directors Association, "wouldn't it be more accurate to see for yourself what happened, what the assistant's demeanor was?" Cochran, whose organization represents electronic journalists in more than 30 countries, believes cameras ensure a more faithful rendering of the facts. "To argue against cameras is to say that we prefer the less accurate version of what happened, that we'd rather have reporters paraphrasing what was said on the stand rather than showing in reality what was said on the stand."

Pat Lalama, who covers cases for "Celebrity Justice," agrees, saying that her ability to be accurate is at stake when cameras are barred. "Judges will say, 'When you guys come into the courtroom, you only show snippets, and you only show the salacious stuff,' and yes, there's some merit to that, let's be honest. But at the same time, if they want us to be able to tell a more complete story, they should let us into the courtroom, and there should be no conditions, except for protecting children or domestic violence victims, etc."

"It should be a free market, so that people can better understand the judicial process and so that we'll have less of a chance to be left to our own devices and take things out of context."

Do cameras in the courtroom offer accuracy or merely a false sense of accuracy?

More Accurate Reporting?

But do cameras in the courtroom offer accuracy or merely a false sense of accuracy? If we were watching real footage of the Peterson trial, we might be tempted to think we have a complete knowledge of the case. But we would be wrong. We are always dependent on the Pat Lalamas and the MSNBC/CNN talking heads of the world, because actual trials don't unfold as concisely as those on "The Practice" [a TV legal drama], where the writers spell out the issues for the viewer.

Most of us need media explication to fully comprehend litigation, just as we have relied on experts to untangle the Byzantine dynamics of the marriage-amendment votes in the Massachusetts House. Indeed, we are always vulnerable to the reporting skills of TV and newspaper journalists, whether it comes to coverage of a war or of the justice system.

Court TV's Graham, who argued unsuccessfully before a Peterson judge to get cameras into the preliminary hearing, says his cause is suffering unfairly due to negative attitudes about reality TV. "It's rubbing off on coverage of trials, and I think it's illogical that it is. 'Reality' television—it's a misnomer, because it's all engineered to be as entertaining as possible. Coverage of trials on TV is the absolute flip side of that, because it's the fly-on-the-wall approach in which everything that happens in that courtroom is shown as if you were sitting there, and nothing is done that would not be done exactly the same way if a camera were not there."

But Court TV is one of the few outlets actually able to provide gavel-to-gavel coverage of celebrity cases. Even when cameras are allowed in the courtroom, most media outlets end up presenting heavily edited versions of the long day's events, with an emphasis on the dishy moments—an approach that isn't as far from the celebrity reality soap "The Surreal Life" as we'd like to think it is.

Electronic Watchdog

Cochran also points out that a camera in the courtroom serves as a monitoring device, especially in a celebrity trial. "The public has every right to see that the celebrity is not getting better treatment than they deserve, but also that the celebrity is not getting worse treatment than they deserve."

Still, there are always people in the courtroom, including reporters in many cases, who are monitoring the proceedings; the trial is public, with or without cameras. Indeed, the presence of a camera could affect the fairness of a celebrity trial as much as its absence, if it inspires lawyers to advertise themselves to a country of potential clients. Cameras don't automatically bring integrity with them.

And really, any ordinary TV viewer who says he or she is watching celebrity trial footage to gauge fairness probably claims to look at *Playboy* or *Playgirl* for the articles. Instead of serving principles of fairness and accuracy, cameras in these trials only serve to promote gossipy entertainment and goose Nielsen ratings. Star cases aren't about the real crimes, the real victims, and the real litigation issues; they're about water-cooler excitement, [late-night TV host] David Letterman gags, [crime writer] Dominick Dunne scandal blather, and 24-hour cable news fodder.

Graham says that if that's true, so what. "It's an elitist notion that the great unwashed shouldn't be permitted to indulge themselves in this sort of tabloid satisfaction," he says. "Abraham Lincoln was the most entertaining trial lawyer in the state of Illinois. People came down and sat and watched old honest Abe try cases. That's in the American tradition. Some people who have loftier values say, 'You shouldn't get your entertainment on such a low level as when someone is accused of killing his wife.' Maybe the people who say that prefer to go to the opera, but other people would rather see a trial. In a democracy, maybe each person should be able to do their own thing."

Ultimately, the cameras in celebrity trials are watching for dollars, not for conscience.

Motives Behind the Camera

And yet, even though I don't like opera, I will cringe watching TV treat the Jackson case or the Blake case with greater urgency than, say, the Sept. 11 commission hearings. When the media staked out the Santa Barbara Municipal Airport for many hours waiting for Jackson to surrender in November, it was a small warning sign of what will happen once the trial starts in earnest. If the Jackson judge continues to keep cameras out of the trial, at least there's some possibility of diminished coverage. As Graham points out, "The coverage of trials and judicial matters is greatly reduced when the camera is not allowed in."

Ultimately, the cameras in celebrity trials are watching for dollars, not for conscience. Media outlets are gung ho to interrupt programming with "Breaking News" featuring Jackson's housekeeper or his security guard, just to keep us tuned in and talking. Me, I'd rather take refuge in TV Land.

12

Beltway Sniper John Allen Muhammad's Trial Should Be Televised

Radio-Television News Directors Association et al.

The authors of this motion include the Radio-Television News Directors Association, the Virginia Association of Broadcasters, ABC, CNN, CBS, Court TV, Fox News, NBC, NEWSCHANNEL 8, WJLA-TV, WRC-TV, WTOP Radio, WTTG TV, W*USA-TV, the Reporters Committee for Freedom of the Press, and the Society of Professional Journalists.

The Movants, who represent members of the electronic media, request permission to cover specific pretrial and trial proceedings in the case of Commonwealth of Virginia vs. John Allen Muhammad, *one of the two suspects in the Beltway sniper attacks of October 2002. Such coverage would grant the public its Constitutional right of access to the trial, which is of particular interest considering the enormous impact the attacks had on the area's citizens. While the print media would inform the American people of the trial's progress, only the electronic media could give the public the opportunity to witness the trial themselves rather than depending on the reports of the print journalists in the courtroom. As long as members of the electronic media conduct themselves in an orderly and rational manner in the courtroom, there is much for the public to gain from the video recording and televising of these trial proceedings.*

Radio-Television News Directors Association et al., Memorandum of Law in Support of Consolidated Motion for Leave to Record and Telecast Proceedings, presented to the Circuit Court for Prince William County, Commonwealth of Virginia, November 19, 2002.

Movants are representatives of the electronic media who seek to cover certain pre-trial and trial proceedings in this case. More broadly, Movants represent the public at large. Our country has an historical commitment to public access to judicial proceedings. The right of a "public" trial belongs not only to the accused, but to the public as well. The public's interest in asserting that right through its surrogate, the press, is particularly compelling in this case.

The October 2002 shooting deaths in Virginia, Maryland, and the District of Columbia profoundly affected a broad cross-section of citizens. These events touched not only the lives of citizens in the D.C. metropolitan area, but also persons throughout the nation, including those directly affected in Alabama, Louisiana, and Washington State. There is a significant need for recording and telecast of these proceedings, because the physical confines of the courtroom and the importance of preserving order and decorum in the courtroom necessarily limit attendance.

As the Virginia General Assembly has recognized, audiovisual coverage of judicial proceedings can be accomplished without prejudice to the parties, and without disruption or distraction. To permit recording and telecast, pursuant to the strict guidelines set forth in the Virginia Code, will serve the public interest in contemporaneous, complete, and objective information about the administration of justice in this case. In countless cases in Virginia, including numerous capital cases, electronic coverage of proceedings has served the public interest in a manner entirely consistent with the fair and uninterrupted administration of justice. . . .

In the Public Interest

As U.S. Attorney General John Ashcroft stated in his November 7, 2002, press conference, announcing the transfer of the defendant to this jurisdiction: "[f]or 23 days in October, our community lived in fear. Killers stalked the national capital area." While the instant case involves a single murder, the crimes alleged touched citizens throughout Virginia, Maryland, and the District of Columbia, in their everyday lives, while sending children to school, filling their cars with gasoline, and shopping at suburban malls. The public interest in these crimes extended far beyond the boundaries of Prince William County to the nation at large.

The nationwide impact of the case broadens the scope of the public interest.

The keen interest of the majority of residents of the D.C. metropolitan area and the nation undoubtedly will persist through the administration of justice in this case. The broad scope of the crimes is reflected in the charges. The Commonwealth's indictment alleges that the defendant engaged in the "commission of or attempted commission of an act of terrorism with the intent to intimidate the civilian population at large." Under this definition, our entire community is the "victim." Moreover, the nationwide impact of the case broadens the scope of the public interest. Government authorities have alleged that this case is linked to other shootings in Alabama, Louisiana, and Washington State. These communities also have a direct interest in seeing the fair administration of justice in the case.

Justice Oliver Wendell Holmes' words of 1884 are still true today: "[i]t is desirable that the trial of cases should take place under the public eye . . . that every citizen should be able to satisfy himself with his own eyes as to the mode in which a public duty is performed." . . . However, the many people touched by these crimes simply cannot attend the court proceedings in person. Today, most citizens learn about the progress of criminal trials not by attending themselves, but through the news media. Accordingly, the United States Supreme Court has recognized the need for access by media representatives, who serve as surrogates for the public. . . .

Electronic Media's Unique Advantages

While both print and electronic media serve that important surrogate role, only the electronic media has the ability to provide the public with a close visual and aural approximation of actually witnessing a trial without physical attendance. The General Assembly, through the enactment of Virginia Code § 19.2-266, and the Virginia Supreme Court, in cases such as *[Southern Pacific Co. v.] Stewart* (1918), . . . have sanctioned meeting the public need for information about judicial proceedings through the vehicle of allowing for their recording and telecast.

Virginia's experience has demonstrated that electronic coverage of court proceedings . . . works to achieve the goals involved.

Permitting electronic coverage here will ensure that the information conveyed is contemporaneous, complete, and objective. Such coverage will convey the evidence as it is received in the courtroom setting—in a rational, dispassionate, and orderly manner. Without a camera in the courtroom as an objective observer, the public will be forced to rely upon the selective summaries of those members of the media who are able to secure a coveted spot in the courtroom. Conversely, electronic coverage of proceedings allows citizens to have a first-hand view of the case as it proceeds under the control of the presiding judge, and allows them to make their own unfiltered assessments. Given the impact of the crimes alleged on the community at large, it is particularly important that, in order to understand whatever verdict is rendered, the same community be able to see and hear the case presented by the prosecution and the defense. As the Supreme Court noted, "[p]eople in an open society do not demand infallibility from their institutions but it [will be] difficult for them to accept what they are prohibited from observing." . . .

Movants seek an order that allows the audio-visual coverage of certain proceedings, consistent with Virginia Code § 19.2-266. Virginia's experience has demonstrated that electronic coverage of court proceedings, pursuant to the statute, works to achieve the goals involved. Recording and telecast of court proceedings preserves the important public rights to access and information, without prejudicing the parties or disrupting the proceedings.

13

Beltway Sniper Lee Boyd Malvo's Trial Should Not Be Televised

Andrew Cohen

Andrew Cohen is chief legal analyst for CBS News and a columnist at the Washington Post.

Fairfax County, Virginia, circuit court judge Jane Marum Roush will probably deny a request for camera access to her courtroom during sniper suspect Lee Boyd Malvo's trial. While the public does have a right to a public trial, a suspect's right to a fair trial must be considered as well. There are already a number of factors that threaten a fair trial for Malvo, such as the publicity of his alleged crime, and cameras in the courtroom would only exacerbate this threat. The court is obligated to protect Malvo from any potentially prejudicial influences, such as cameras. If the media want cameras in the courtroom during Malvo's trial, they will need to convince Judge Roush that they will not increase prejudice toward Malvo in the courtroom, which will be very difficult for them to do.

Young sniper suspect Lee Boyd Malvo has enough going against him these days without having to worry about cameras televising his Virginia trial to a nation still bitter about last fall's [2002] shooting spree [after which Malvo and John Allen Muhammad were accused of murdering ten people and injuring three others]. That's essentially why Fairfax

County Circuit Court Judge Jane Marum Roush will almost certainly deny a cameras-in-court request made [January 30, 2003,] by several media organizations, including my beloved CBS.

It's true, as the media consortium argues, that the "right of a 'public trial' belongs not only to the accused, but to the public as well." But it's also true that no one at Court TV will be going to death row if things don't go well for the defense at the capital trial. . . .

The balancing test that all judges must consider when evaluating a request to televise a trial simply doesn't balance out in favor of courtroom cameras in this case. In fact, since Malvo's attorneys object to the notion of a televised trial, I'm not sure it's even a particularly close call.

Even without cameras, it's going to be difficult to give the juvenile defendant a fair trial before an impartial jury. The sniper shootings probably have generated more publicity than any other crimes since the Oklahoma City [federal building] bombing in 1995 [in which 168 were killed and 800 wounded].

What's more, the shootings took place near the epicenter of governmental power and were covered by the nation's media elite, many of whom lived in communities directly affected by attacks. And, once Malvo goes to trial, the people who will be asked to judge him dispassionately as the "conscience of the community" are the very same people who were both terrified (thinking they'd be the next random target) and/or inconvenienced (mostly by those traffic dragnets) . . . during the shooting spree.

Televising the trial may make sense in ordinary cases but is a terrible idea in this case.

Problems for Malvo

Indeed, the very randomness and expanse of the "crime" scene—much of Virginia and Maryland, for starters—creates a "personalized" attachment to the case for both the trial's main actors (the lawyers, witnesses and jurors) and its bit players (the reporters and the general public).

This is a foundational problem for Malvo that makes it all the more vital for the court to protect him from any non-organic emotional overheating. Standing alone, this volatile pre-trial atmosphere ought to be worrisome enough to convince Judge Roush that televising the trial may make sense in ordinary cases but is a terrible idea in this case.

But there are other reasons why the deck is stacked against Malvo to the extent that televising his trial might push the whole case into Leopold-and-Loeb territory [i.e., reminiscent of the 1924 murder trial of two wealthy college students, Nathan Leopold and Richard Loeb, who retained famous defense attorney Clarence Darrow, turning the trial into a national media event]. First, Malvo faces capital murder charges in a jurisdiction specifically handpicked to ensure the best chance that he will be executed if he's convicted. Prosecutors have been very candid about why they chose Virginia and what they expect Malvo's jurors to do. Second, law enforcement officials have been improperly leaking information about the case against him in order to further influence potential jurors before the evidence starts coming in.

Some trials are simply too tightly wound, too hyper-charged to digest the additional element of televised coverage.

Third, there have not been additional sniper attacks since Malvo and his alleged cohort John Allen Muhammed were arrested—a point that will surely come up at trial if it is still applicable. And, fourth, even if Malvo somehow gets a favorable result in this upcoming trial, he faces the possibility of at least six more murder trials, any one of which can result in either a life sentence or his execution. And it's this probability of successive trials—first Virginia, then Maryland, then maybe Alabama and the District of Columbia—that gives the defense its best argument against cameras.

A Unique Case

Whatever a televised Malvo trial would do to the participants in that trial, allowing Americans to watch the trial from the comfort of their homes surely would make it a lot harder to get an impartial jury for the next Malvo trial, or the Malvo trial after that. Indeed, it is the very hopelessness of Malvo's legal future that gives his present attorneys an argument against cameras that most defendants don't have.

The folks who want cameras in the courtroom ultimately will have to convince Judge Roush that there will be no direct prejudice to Malvo in her courtroom but also that there will be no increased potential for prejudice in someone else's courtroom during a subsequent Malvo trial. I think that's an impossible hurdle for the news organizations to overcome.

Some trials ought to be televised and news organizations ought to push whenever and wherever they can for more access to courtrooms. But some trials are simply too tightly wound, too hyper-charged to digest the additional element of televised coverage. Besides, people who want to appreciate the "public" nature of the Malvo trial will still have plenty of opportunities. The courtroom door will be open to the general public.

Media types like myself will hang on every word and report what we see and hear. There will be daily transcripts available online. In short, no one who wants to know what's happening inside Judge Roush's courtroom will be left lacking for information.

Organizations to Contact

The editors have compiled the following list of organizations concerned with the issues debated in this book. The descriptions are derived from materials provided by the organizations. All have publications or information available for interested readers. The list was compiled on the date of publications of the present volume; the information provided here may change. Be aware that many organizations may take several weeks or longer to respond to inquiries, so allow as much time as possible.

American Bar Association (ABA)
321 N. Clark St., Chicago, IL   60610
(312) 988-5000
Web site: www.abanet.org

The ABA is a professional organization representing the legal profession. It provides continuing legal education for lawyers and judges and promotes excellence within the legal system. Its publications include the *ABA Journal*.

American Judicature Society (AJS)
The Opperman Center at Drake University
Des Moines, IA   50311
(515) 271-2281 • fax: (515) 279-3090
Web site: www.ajs.org

The AJS is a nonpartisan organization that represents judges, lawyers, and other citizens concerned about the administration of justice. The society works to uphold the independence and integrity of the courts, and promotes public understanding of the justice system. AJS publishes the bimonthly magazine, *Judicature*, the quarterly *Judicial Conduct Reporter*, and numerous reports, handbooks, videos, and books.

Fairness and Accuracy in Reporting (FAIR)
112 W. Twenty-seventh St., New York, NY   10001
(212) 633-6700 • fax: (212) 727-7668
e-mail: fair@fair.org
Web site: www.fair.org

FAIR is a national media watch group that exposes media bias and censorship. It advocates for greater diversity in the press and scrutinizes media practices that marginalize minority and dissenting viewpoints. FAIR publishes the magazine *Extra!* as well as periodic Action Alerts and broadcasts the weekly radio program *Counter Spin.*

Federal Judicial Center
Thurgood Marshall Federal Judiciary Bldg.
Washington, DC   20002-8003
(202) 502-4000
Web site: www.fjc.gov

The Federal Judicial Center is the federal judicial system's research and education agency. It offers continuing education and training for federal judges, researches federal judicial procedures and court operations, and develops recommendations for the operation of the federal courts. The center publishes various educational materials such as videos and an annual report.

First Amendment Center
1207 Eighteenth Ave. South, Nashville, TN   37212
(615) 727-1600 • fax: (615) 727-1319
e-mail: info@fac.org
Web site: www:firstamendmentcenter.org

The First Amendment Center is an education and advocacy organization devoted to the preservation and protection of the First Amendment, including freedoms of speech, religion, and the press. It has an office in Arlington, Virginia, affiliated with the Freedom Forum, and an office in Nashville, Tennessee, affiliated with Vanderbilt University. Its publications include the annual *State of the First Amendment* report.

Joan Shorenstein Center on the Press, Politics & Public Policy

John F. Kennedy School of Government
Cambridge, MA   02138
(617) 495-8269 • fax: (617) 495-8696
Web site: www.ksg.harvard.edu/presspol/index.htm

The Joan Shorenstein Center on the Press, Politics & Public Policy is a research organization that explores the intersections of the press, politics, and public policy. The center focuses on the role the media play in society, particularly how they affect U.S. politics and policy. The center publishes papers and reports such as *Foreign News Coverage: The US Media's Undervalued Asset* and *The Reporter's Privilege, Then and Now*, and an annual newsletter, *Press/Politics*.

National Association of Criminal Defense Lawyers (NACDL)

1150 Eighteenth St. NW, Ste. 950, Washington, DC   20036
(202) 872-8600 • fax: (202) 872-8690
e-mail: assist@nacdl.org
Web site: www.nacdl.org

The NACDL is a professional bar association representing criminal defense lawyers. The organization works to ensure justice and due process for defendants and to preserve fairness within the criminal justice system. The NACDL publishes an e-newsletter, *NACDL E-News*, and periodic press releases.

National Freedom of Information Coalition (NFOIC)

Missouri School of Journalism, Columbia, MO   65211
(573) 882-5736 • fax: (573) 884-6204
e-mail: cdavis@nfoic.org
Web site: www.nfoic.org

NFOIC is an organization dedicated to protecting citizens' right to oversee their government. It supports citizen-run and state-level First Amendment organizations, facilitates the exchange of information, and researches and provides information on freedom of information issues. It publishes the e-newsletter, *FOI Advocate*.

Pew Research Center for the People and the Press

1615 L St. NW, Washington, DC 20036
(202) 419-4350 • fax: (202) 419-4399
e-mail: info@people-press.org
Web site: http://people-press.org

The Pew Research Center for the People and the Press is an independent research group that studies attitudes toward the press as well as political and public policy issues. The center conducts national surveys measuring public response to major news stories and serves as an important source of information for journalists, scholars, and political leaders. It publishes survey reports such as *Internet News Audience Highly Critical of News Organizations: Views of Press Values and Performance, 1985–2007* and *Public Knowledge of Current Affairs Little Changed by News and Information Revolutions: What Americans Know, 1989–2007*.

Radio-Television News Directors Association (RTNDA)

1600 K St. NW, Ste. 700, Washington, DC 20006-2838
(202) 659-6510 • fax: (202) 223-4007
Web site: www.rtnda.org

RTNDA is the world's largest electronic news professional organization, with more than three thousand members. It is devoted to maintaining a standard of excellence in electronic journalism. RTNDA's publications include *Communicator: The Magazine for Electronic Journalists* and *Cameras in the Court: A State-by-State Guide*.

Reporters Committee for Freedom of the Press (RCFP)

1101 Wilson Blvd., Ste. 1100, Arlington, VA 22209
(800) 336-4243
e-mail: rcfp.@rcf.org
Web site: www.rcfp.org

The RCFP is a nonprofit organization created in 1970 to protect reporters' rights. It provides information about free speech issues and advocates for journalists' interests, such as keeping sources confidential. The committee publishes the quarterly magazine the *News Media and the Law* in addition to *The Open Government Guide: Secret Justice*, a series of reports about access to the U.S. judicial system, and numerous other publications.

Society of Professional Journalists (SPJ)
Eugene S. Pulliam National Journalism Center
Indianapolis, IN 46208
(317) 927-8000 • fax: (317) 920-4789
Web site: www.spj.org

The Society of Professional Journalists is an organization that promotes high standards of professional ethics, provides professional development, and advocates for the rights of journalists as guaranteed by the First Amendment. SPJ publications include the *Quill: A Magazine for the Professional Journalist*, the *Journalist* magazine, and *SPJ Leads*.

Bibliography

Books

David S. Allen	*Democracy, Inc.: The Press and Law in the Corporate Rationalization of the Public Sphere*, Champaign: University of Illinois Press, 2005.
Lawrence Baum	*Judges and Their Audiences: A Perspective on Judicial Behavior.* Princeton, NJ: Princeton University Press, 2006.
Randall P. Bezanson	*How Free Can the Free Press Be?* Champaign: University of Illinois Press, 2003.
Jon Bruschke and William Earl Loges	*Free Press vs. Fair Trials: Examining Publicity's Role in Trial Outcomes*, Mahwah, NJ: Lawrence Erlbaum, 2003.
Marjorie Cohn and David Dow	*Cameras in the Courtroom: Television and the Pursuit of Justice.* Lanham, MD: Rowman & Littlefield, 2002.
Mona Shafer Edwards	*Captured! Inside the World of Celebrity Trials.* Santa Monica, CA: Santa Monica Press, 2006.
Richard L. Fox, Robert W. Van Sickel, Thomas L. Steiger	*Tabloid Justice: Criminal Justice in an Age of Media Frenzy.* 2nd ed. Boulder, CO: Lynne Rienner, 2007.

Nancy Grace   *Objection! How High-Priced Defense Attorneys, Celebrity Defendants, and a 24/7 Media Have Highjacked Our Criminal Justice System.* New York: Hyperion, 2005.

Yvonne Jewkes   *Media and Crime.* Thousand Oaks, CA: Sage, 2004.

Eric Louw   *The Media and the Political Process.* Thousand Oaks, CA: Sage, 2007.

Paul Mason   *Criminal Visions: Media Representations of Crime and Justice.* Cullompton, UK: Willan, 2004.

Roslyn Muraskin and Shelly Feuer Domash   *Crime and the Media: Headlines vs. Reality.* Upper Saddle River, NJ: Prentice Hall, 2006.

Hedieh Nasheri   *Crime and Justice in the Age of Court TV.* New York: LFB, 2002.

Ray Surette   *Media, Crime, and Criminal Justice: Images, Realities, and Policies.* Belmont, CA: Wadsworth, 2006.

David A. Yalof   *The First Amendment and the Media in the Court of Public Opinion.* New York: Cambridge University Press, 2002.

Periodicals

Karen Aho   "Television and the Supreme Court," *Columbia Journalism Review,* September/October 2003.

Al Baker   "Ruling Upholds Ban on Cameras in Court," *New York Times*, June 17, 2005.

Robert Barnes   "A Renewed Call to Televise the Supreme Court," *Washington Post*, February 12, 2007.

Joan Biskupic   "Justice Pleads with Senate: No Cameras in High Court," *USA Today*, February 15, 2007.

Kevin Brass   "Trial and Error?" *American Journalism Review*, April/May 2004.

Andrew Brenner   "Courtrooms Shuttered to Cameras in Three Trials," *News Media and the Law*, Spring 2005.

Broadcasting & Cable "Cameras Belong in Court," June 20, 2005.

Broadcasting & Cable "Let the Sunshine In," September 19, 2005.

Amanda Buck   "Shuttered Justice," *News Media and the Law*, Winter 2006.

Amanda Buck   "Would Cameras Change the Court?" *News Media and the Law*, Spring 2006.

Kathy Chang   "Focusing on Courts," *News Media and the Law*, Fall 2004.

Steve Chapman   "Should the Revolution Be Televised?" *Slate*, January 23, 2002.

Eric Deggans
"Michael Jackson's Molestation Case: The Blob That Ate Media Credibility," *St. Petersburg (FL) Times*, January 11, 2004.

Bill Delmore
"Cameras in the Courtoom: Limited Access Only," *Texas Bar Journal*, October 2004.

Jan E. DuBois
"Keep Cameras Out," *USA Today*, December 8, 2005.

Bob Egelko
"Specter Trial Renews Debate on TV in Courtroom," *San Francisco Chronicle*, April 25, 2007.

Eddie Florek, Rebecca Daugherty, and Kirsten B. Mitchell
"Camera Controversy in Courtroom Continues," *News Media and the Law*, Winter 2005.

Dan Glaister
"Media Coverage Stifled by Judge," *Guardian* (UK), June 13, 2005.

Liam Hurtley
"High-Profile Cases Bring Attention to Media's Struggle for Greater Camera Access to Courts," *News Media and the Law*, Winter 2004.

Tom Jackman
"Balancing Acts Need Not Tilt Toward Secrecy," *News Media and the Law*, Spring 2004.

Peter Johnson
"Court TV Pushes for Wider Camera Access in Courtrooms," *USA Today*, October 6, 2004.

Jane Kirtley — "Taming the Media Circus," *American Journalism Review*, October/November 2003.

Dahlia Lithwick — "The Letterman Justice," *Slate*, December 8, 2005.

Dahlia Lithwick — "Off the Bench," *New York Times*, August 29, 2004.

Dahlia Lithwick — "We Won't Get O.J.-ed Again," *Slate*, June 9, 2004.

Bob Marshall-Andrews — "Court on Camera," *New Statesman*, February 16, 2004.

Boyce F. Martin Jr. — "Gee Whiz, the Sky Is Falling!" *Michigan Law Review First Impressions*, vol. 106, 2007.

New York Times — "Cameras in the Courts," May 15, 2007.

New York Times — "What Every Iraqi Should See," March 16, 2006.

George Parnham — "Cameras in the Courtroom: Whenever Possible," *Texas Bar Journal*, October 2004.

Mark J. Pescatore — "Are Supreme Court Cameras Necessary?" *Government Video*, December 2005.

Quill — "An Open Question," November 14, 2005.

Tejal Shah — "Courting Camera Access," *News Media and the Law*, Summer 2004.

Catherine Spratt   "Court TV," *News Media and the Law*, Winter 2007.

Seth Stern   "Televised Trials: Terror Compounds Debate," *Christian Science Monitor*, January 9, 2002.

Tom Sullivan   "New York High Court Says Camera Ban Constitutional," *News Media and the Law*, Summer 2005.

Tina Susman   "Wheels of Justice Turn Secretly," *Newsday*, June 13, 2005.

Kaitlin Thaney   "Senator Pushes for Cameras in High Court," *News Media and the Law*, Fall 2005.

Al Tompkins   "No Time Like the Present," *News Media and the Law*, Winter 2007.

USA Today   "Let Public See Justice at Work," December 8, 2005.

Richard Zoglin   "Remember Televised Trials?" *Time*, February 14, 2005.

Index